LIVING YOUR
PURPOSE

Endosements

I was really moved and inspired after reading Living Your Purpose. It helped me redefine my purpose and refocus on what's really important in life: Football, motorcycles and beer. The stories in this book will give you exactly what you need to start living your life with purpose and passion. Please buy it because they owe me money, thanks!

Andy Dooley
Creator of Vibration Activation™
Expert on LOA, Vibration coach and comedian
Andydooley.com

The sharing of personal stories has always been the way of imparting wisdom and learning from experience. The stories in this book are about Creators who have faced challenges (or Challengers) and the fire of the human experience, only to emerge more focused and more purposeful in living their lives. They are truly reflective of what it means to live on purpose.

David Emerald
Author, *The Power of TED* (*The Empowerment Dynamic)*

In reading the stories of each author's path to finding themselves, you will start to find you. There isn't one way that fits everyone; there is just the way that is right for you. Somehow in the process of reading these writers' unique ways, yours will emerge, and you will know it with that the quiet, clear certainty that intuition first uses to introduce itself. You need only recognize it and honor it. Trust it one time and it will grow stronger into clarity that glows with its own brightness, and you will no longer struggle to hear it or know it. It will only be up to you to decide if you want to honor it.

Susan Echols

This book could not have come about at a better time. What an inspiration for the path I am currently traveling. It's as if a portal has opened and my mind is open to much more than messages "seen," "heard," "spoken"... at least by me, personally. What better affirmation about the changes going on within us, or the world, than this very book. Expressively written by those that have made significant changes to their lives and filled with inspiration for anyone reading this book to see the possibilities of how life can be more meaningful for themselves.

Peg Dienhart, LMT NCTMB
Timeless Touch Massage
Germantown & Mequon, Wisconsin

Living Your Purpose is an inspiring book. A worthwhile addition to your personal library! These stories help remind us how powerful this life can be!

Troy Parkinson
Medium and Author of *Bridge to the Afterlife*
www.troyparkinson.com

LIVING YOUR
PURPOSE

Living Your Purpose

The authors of this book do not dispense medical advice or prescribe the use of any technique as a form of treatment for physical or medical problems without the advice of a physician, either directly, or indirectly. If the reader chooses to use any of the information in this book, the author and publisher assume no responsibility for their actions.

Ordering information: Quantity Sales. Special discounts are available on quantity purchases by corporations, associations, and others. For details, contact the "Special Sales Department at Visionary Insight Press."

Visionary Insight Press, LLC, P.O. Box 30484, Spokane, WA 99223

Visionary Insight Press, the Visionary Insight Press logo and its individual parts are trademarks of Visionary Insight Press, LLC

Compiled by: Nancy A. Newman and Lisa A. Hardwick
Editorial Director: Nancy Newman
Project Director: Lisa Hardwick
Cover Design and Photos of Ms. Johnston: Kris Voelker
Back cover photo credit: Nancy Newman by Kent Henderson, Paula Obeid by Portrait Innovations, Shanda Bisanz by Mark Bailey, Kim Richardson by Karen Shell/Shell Photographics, Kailah Eglington by Derek George Photography, Liana Salas by Kris Voelker, Marci Cagen by Shaunna M. O'Dowd, April L. Dodd by Nicole Ryan Photography, Cris Hitterman by Portrait Innovations, Nicole Stevenson by Christy D. Swanberg Photography, Dawn Amberley by Karen Seargeant, Jodie Harvala by Abby Tow, Shellie Couch by Deb Hagen Photography & Digital Art, Sandra J. Filer by Kim Coffman, Alan Michael by Ron Erhardt, Kim Pratte by Angie Nemanic/Reflective Images, Jody Kratz by James Kratz, Tammy Gynell Lagoski by David Vernon, and Lisa Hardwick by Jenny Paul.

A ship is safe in
the harbor, but
that's not what
ships are for.

~ WILLIAM SHEDD

Table of Contents

Foreword
by Laura Alden Kamm

At some point in time, we all raise our hearts to the sky and plead for the answer to the most profound existential question we could ever ask: For what purpose was I born?

During my late teens, many of my friends knew what they were going to study at college. I knew that I needed to go to college; but that is as far as it went. My path in life was blank. One blustery, fleshing-chilling day, I sat high up on the bleachers in the vast and empty bowl of The Ohio State University stadium with a friend. His name was Jack.

Jack and I came from the same small town high school; in fact, he sat in front of me in homeroom through our entire high school years. That day in the stadium, my emotions matched the grey November sky. As Jack and I talked, he handed me a poem he had written about me. The core of the poem was that someday, the light inside of me would shine brightly. Even though I could not see the light in this moment, I would find my way in the not so distant future. I would know who I am, and what I am here to do.

What was true for me that day is true for all of us. To wander without personal clarity throughout your life can, at times, feel excruciating, boring, or numbing. The solution to that pain is to discover your authentic self. Such a journey will guide you to your path of service and what you are here to offer the world – your purpose. It may feel like a daunting task to know your truest self and purpose; however, discovering your reason for being may not be as hard as you believe.

You might say that all sounds well and good, but how do I do this? What will happen in the process? Will I be okay? Will I be able to make money when I find my purpose? In fact, does everyone really have a purpose? Is there a divine plan? Or is our life a series of random events chaotically thrown together without rhyme or reason? These are all necessary questions that beg your soul to release the answers. Keep asking them.

You were created and equipped for this adventure, or you wouldn't be asking these questions. You would be content and compliant with whatever life brought your way. As you take a positive approach to this soulful search by eliciting your intuition and using your power of reason, you'll find your purpose. How? By diving into self-discovery, where the awakening to your purpose will naturally occur.

By the time I reached my mid-twenties I thought I had found my path. I was studying to be an architect. On Super Bowl Sunday in 1982, I became very ill. Within eleven days I went blind and died in an ambulance as it transported me from one hospital to another. At the time, I was a mother of two charming toddlers, a wife, and a student. Yet, I had shut down my childhood gifts of intuition and spiritual connection. I was doing my best to fit in and was living what I thought was a normal life. However, with the advent of my death experience and journey to the other side, I recaptured the truths of my life and true purpose.

I learned many things on the other side that have become the cornerstones of my life and my life's work. Needless, to say, no matter what I thought my calling was – architecture – it morphed into my true purpose. I have become an intuitive expert and architect of energy and the many forms it takes in our lives. Who knew, right?

My point is this. Everything that I have done, every step I have taken (whether it seemed to work out as I had planned or not) mattered. I know you understand this, as the same is true for you, too.

Your life's purpose exists because you, too, exist. Your purpose is alive, even if you're not clear what it is or how to offer it to the world. Your purpose is still there, alive within you. You're quietly being *it*. Even if you don't have all of the pieces put together yet, be comforted by the fact that your purpose is within you. This is true because you are alive, here and now.

In the past, perhaps, you've been waiting for someone to tell you what your purpose is. That can be a long wait; especially if there is no self-investigation. You have to be the one stirring the pot and waking yourself up. Your purpose-filled life is like a magnificent stained glass window – each brilliant piece adds color and perspective, coming from your personal convictions, values, and inner truth.

Life is certainly a process of self-discovery and understanding; nonetheless, we all need guidance and a supportive witness now and then. This is the purpose of this book – *Living Your Purpose*.

The pages that follow will stir your heart and awaken the light within you. The light you are here to carry will shine in a dazzling, undeniable way. It cannot help but do so. No longer will you need to beg your soul for the breadcrumbs that take you into that knowing. Your purpose and the inner peace that follows will show itself.

Try this simple prayer, "God, what can I do for you today?" This simple question cast out into the void will change your life, and it will reveal your purpose over time. It is always up to you to make the most of your life. After asking this question and reveling in the wisdom contained in this book, I am confident you will find an enriched and purposeful life.

May the words on these pages be a blessing in your life, as your heart-felt purpose will surely be a blessing to others.

Laura Alden Kamm
Speaker ~ Author ~ Expert Medical and Structural Intuitive and Medium ~ Near-death Experiencer

Author of:
Practical Advice From Angels™ (A New and Inspiring Series ~ Summer 2013)
Intuitive Wellness; using your body's inner wisdom to heal
Unlocking Your Intuitive Power; how to read the energy of anything
Color Intuition; master the energy of color for higher awareness, extraordinary perception, and healing

www.LauraAldenKamm.com
www.energymedicine.org

Introduction

By Sunny Dawn Johnston

What is my purpose? That is probably one of the top five questions I am asked when teaching or counseling. My students ask: "What am I meant to do, who am I meant to be? What do I need to do to serve my purpose?" I often respond that MY purpose, YOUR purpose, and/or OUR purpose is to simply just BE ... To BE, in whatever form that is for you. Purpose is constantly changing as we grow and evolve, therefore the form purpose takes in your life, is ever changing.

In my life, my purpose was not always clear to me. For many years, I felt as if I had no purpose. When I was a single mom, on welfare, it was hard to see. I felt miserable and sad that I had missed my life's calling. Many nights, I flipped through my empty wallet, while my first born lay on the floor wrapped in a pile of blankets because I didn't have any heat. In the midst of that, I was certain I was not living my purpose.

Looking back on my life now, I can see how that experience and all of my feelings were indeed a part of my purpose. And today I know my purpose is to BE LOVE.

This book is about purpose and each individual's perception and experiences of purpose. There is no right or wrong. Each author will share their perceptions, their discoveries and their insights into purpose.

A final question I will leave you with ... what you are doing to LIVE in purpose today?

www.sunnydawnjohnston.com

When you are born, your work is placed in your heart. So, what is your work? Your purpose? Are you living it out the way your heart urges you to?

~ KAHLIL GIBRAN

Sunny Dawn Johnston

SUNNY DAWN JOHNSTON is an inspirational speaker, a compassionate spiritual teacher, an internationally acclaimed psychic medium and author of the bestselling book, *Invoking the Archangels - A Nine-Step Process to Heal Your Body, Mind and Soul*. In 2003, Sunny founded Sunlight Alliance, LLC, a spiritual teaching and healing center in Glendale, Arizona where she teaches classes via online streaming all over the world. Her classes and workshops have been called Intensive, Intimate, and Healing. She truly is a Wayshower for the Universal Oneness and Unconditional Love that we all strive for. Sunny is on the faculty at *OMEGA Institute*, *The Infinity Foundation* and a featured speaker at *Celebrate Your Life*. She also volunteers her time as a psychic investigator for the international organization *FIND ME*. This is a non-profit organization of psychic, investigative, and canine search-and-rescue volunteers, working together to provide leads to law enforcement and families of missing persons and homicide victims.

Sunny lives in the sunshine of the Arizona desert with her husband, Brett, sons, Crew and Arizona, and their two dogs, Pelé and Xena. To learn more about Sunny's work, see videos, and read articles, please go to her website.

www.sunnydawnjohnston.com

❧ Living Your Purpose

Listen from within
the song of today
will soon become
the dance of tomorrow

~ SHALAMA VIA SOLARA SKYE

"*What is my purpose?*" This question has been asked for thousands of years, by millions of people of all ages, races and backgrounds. What is my purpose? This book will give you the opportunity to answer that question for yourself. It is an attempt to help you understand not only what your life purpose is, but also to inspire you to live your life consciously, with purpose, each and every day. This book has been woven with stories of determination, passion and hope. Within these pages are examples of what purpose means to a variety of people from different walks of life. From the artist to the stay-at-home mom, the realtor to the psychic and the nurse to the CEO, the journey of discovering and living their purpose is inspiring and life changing.

When I was a child, I felt ... no, I knew that I had a BIG purpose. I knew that I had big shoes to fill. I just "felt" it deep within me. I remember when I was six or seven years old, being in school, and the teacher asked us what we wanted to be when we grew up. Many of the girls wanted to be a wife and a mother, that was their dream. Some of the girls wanted to be a secretary, a teacher, or a nurse. One or two of the girls said, "a lawyer," and were looked at as if to say, "Really? YOU think YOU can BE that?"

When it was my turn to answer the question, I remember wanting to say The President, and I actually wrote it on my paper for class. But I wouldn't say it out loud to the class or even to the teacher. Instead, I too, said the standard "safe" answer: A teacher. It was a good second choice, and it allowed me to fit in with everyone else's answers, too.

One time, a few years later, when asked the same question (and feeling especially brave), I remember verbalizing my "real" answer: "The President." It was at that point that I remember everyone in class looking at me as if I had two heads. "A girl can't be President," they said. And although I felt as though I could do or be anything I wanted to be ... I agreed. They then waited for me to share my real answer, and I again answered: "A teacher." This seemed to be the "right" answer, and made everyone else comfortable, and now, I would again, sort of fit in. These experiences were the beginning of a pattern in my life that spanned over 20 years and manifested into many false beliefs about myself, my value in the world and created many self-induced heartbreaks.

As a little girl, I was very perceptive, wise you might even say. There were some things I just "knew." I didn't know how or why I "knew" them, I just did. As I look back over my life, the following truths became my reality after much resistance, fear, and denial. I believe these truths can and do apply to anyone and, dare I say, everyone.

TRUTH #1: I can do or be anything I want.

I can be anything I want to be. This is true. I can ... and I have. So can you! When I was a young girl, my dad would tell me over and over again that I could do or be anything I wanted ... anything. And, when

I was young, I believed him. He always assured me, even to the point of yelling it when I was being self-critical or playing small. It is one of the greatest gifts he gave to me.

TRUTH #2: I have Purpose.

As a very little girl, I knew I had purpose. I was confident, self-assured, and I knew who I was and my value in the world. I believe that everyone that has come into physical being has purpose. How could we not? WE ARE ALL SPIRIT EMBODIED. We chose to come here and to experience this life in order to expand our consciousness. So, we are all here "on purpose." As random as life may seem sometimes, we all have purpose. And, as unaware as we can be of our purpose at particular times in our lives, that does not negate the fact that we have purpose.

TRUTH #3: My purpose is always being served.

This one took me a little longer to understand completely. I didn't totally grasp what it meant, but at the age of eight, my favorite saying was: "What goes around comes around." I now know that it was laying a foundation for me to understand this truth. Everything that has ever happened in my life has happened for a reason. Whether I understand the reason, like the reason, hate the reason, or don't really care, it has happened for a reason. That reason, is part of my purpose. It may not be a HUGE part of it, but it is a part of it nonetheless.

In this physical world, if you change one thing, one very simple thing, you change everything. Therefore, when you talk about purpose, EVERYTHING becomes a part of the whole, and YOU are the blessed creator of it. Isn't that GREAT to know? You are creating and manifesting your life, therefore your purpose, one minute at a time. We don't always see how the little things are creating the bigger things, but they are all connected. All connected.

Is Purpose Defined by the Individual?
Is It Different for Each Person?

Purpose, to me, is within each person. It is the guidance of the soul. It is something that is innate. A goal on the other hand, is external, and is the guidance of the ego. The expression of purpose is constantly changing. It is an ongoing evolution of our souls, in physical form. As we know, we are spiritual beings having and creating this human experience. Because we are energy, which is ever changing, we, too, are ever changing. Therefore, the purpose within us would be expressed as a constant change of energy in motion.

What Does Purpose Look Like?

There are many ways that my purpose expresses itself in my life. I believe that at any given moment, if I am listening to my heart and my guidance, I am serving my purpose. And, here is the kicker: Even if I am not listening to my heart and guidance, my purpose is still being served. This can be the hard part to understand. Purpose is who we are, not what we do. It shows up under different roles, jobs, acts, words, etc. But there is no end to our purpose. We don't just arrive there one day. With each breath we take, I believe, we are, in fact, living our purpose. The question is, are we living it consciously or unconsciously?

Some days, my purpose shows itself by being a mom. Other days by teaching. It shows up in the variety of roles I play in my life such as being a wife, a friend, a counselor, a daughter, a sister, a medium, an aunt, a cousin, a psychic and so on. Some days my purpose expresses itself through all of my roles (that's a really busy day), other days, it can be hard to tell. I am sure you have days like this, too. Purpose is always moving through me, in all of the ways, and all of the roles in which I express myself. Some days it is clear, absolute, evident ... other days maybe not as much, but it is always there because it is within me. I am always living my purpose. Each and every day in each and every experience, my purpose is being served. Sometimes, I am conscious of how I am serving my purpose, and sometimes I am not. I believe everything happens for a reason, so there has to be purpose in it. And the purpose is sometimes hard to find. Let's explore a couple of experiences where **LESSONS** in purpose occurred. Each were revealed as everyday events as my life naturally unfolded. They each showed up in a different way than maybe you would expect, which is often the case with purpose.

☙ Experience: BE Present

I was six weeks into my fifth pregnancy when I began spotting. Because I had struggled with each and every prior pregnancy, resulting in the loss of three children, the doctors prescribed immediate bed rest. They also prescribed some hormone support to help me carry this pregnancy to term. After three months of bed rest, we were out of the scary zone and into the second trimester, and baby and I seemed to be very healthy. At 19 weeks we were scheduled to have an ultrasound to make sure the baby was healthy and to hopefully discover the sex of the baby as well.

When my mother and I arrived at the doctor's office (my husband wanted the sex to be a secret, so I decided to find out and keep it a secret, and my mom joined me instead), we sat down and waited with baited breath and butterfly stomachs. You see I had one son, seven years old at this time, and throughout the loss of the three previous babies, I had wished, dreamt of, and desperately wanted a girl. My son was a handful, or 10 handfuls, depending on the day, and I thought a girl would be different, which made me want a girl even more.

So, as we sat in the doctor's office impatiently waiting our turn, I grew increasingly nervous. The angels started showing me signs. They began when I noticed this beautiful blond, curly-haired toddler, playing on the floor with a bunch of toys. From a distance, you couldn't tell if it was a boy or girl, just a smiling, happy-go-lucky, blonde curly-haired beauty, but upon further investigation, I could see that it was a boy. He was playing so calmly, quietly – something I had rarely experienced in over seven years with my son, Crew. I sat watching him play and just observed how adorable he was with all of his curls.

As I sat there watching, I heard my mom, who was sitting on the opposite side of me than the little boy, say: "You are going to have one just like that." When I heard her words, I turned to ask her why she would say that, and when I did, she wasn't there. I sat with an awareness in that moment, oh boy, they are forewarning me. I am having a boy. Tears welled up in my eyes as the thought of raising two boys sent me into a tailspin. I was certain I couldn't live through another child like my first one and at that time, all I could think of was: "Oh no."

A few minutes later, my mom sat down next to me, and I shared with her what just happened, and what I thought she told me, although she was nowhere to be found, that I was going to have one just like that. My mom's response now was: "Oh boy, Sunny, they are trying to prepare you."

I argued in my own head: "No, it doesn't mean anything, it's just a little kid playing blocks." As I sat deep in thought, I was startled back to reality by my name being called: "Sunny Dawn Johnston, we are ready for you." Oh boy, I sure hope I am ready for you, I thought.

As we walked into the ultrasound room, we were met by a quiet, but friendly woman. She asked me a few questions about my history, told me what to expect, and what they were looking for. All very normal. As someone who had four previous pregnancies, two ending in miscarriage (one a medical termination, and one a high risk pregnancy), I could repeat the spiel word for word, and as she talked, I faded in and out, listening and not. I already knew what she was going to say. I was confident with the health of the baby, I knew it was healthy. It was the sex that I really wanted confirmation on. Although I already knew, based on my experience in the waiting room, I needed confirmation.

So, she began the ultrasound and small talk at the same time. "How has the pregnancy been for you?" "Great now," I said. "It was scary in the beginning, but we are good now." She asked us what sex we thought the baby was. My mom and I, both still in denial of the message we had just received, said a girl. And then there was silence. Lots of silence. And then she asked the question. The one I will never forget. The one that reminds me over and over again, how everyone is intuitive, even if they don't know it. She asked: "What are you going to name it? If it is a girl, what will her name be?" I said instantly and excitedly, "Sapphire Skye." She continued moving the ultrasound wand all over my tummy, as our conversation continues. "Oh, that is such a pretty name. And, if it is a boy?" With the excitement melting a bit, I said "Arizona."

Then it happened ... she asked me, out of the blue [pun intended] if I were going to name him Arizona Blue. My mom and I both gasped, at the same time. "Why did you ask that?" we said, at the same time ... and she responded, a little embarrassed, "Did that actually come out of my mouth? I've been doing ultrasounds for 17 years, and I have never done that before. I don't know where it came from." Then, as we were sitting there shocked, me knowing that meant that it was a boy, and he was delivering his name to me via this radiologist ... she said: "Well, it looks like Arizona Blue to me," and promptly pointed to the area that showed that he was indeed, a boy! Unbeknownst to the radiologist, we had been vacillating between middle names for a boy, and one of them was Blue.

❧ Lesson:

My purpose, in this particular story, was to be present and listen. First to listen to what I believe my angels and guides were telling me in the waiting room: "You are going to have a boy, and he will be just like this one." This would put my mind at ease over the next five months where I may have been in fear of what was to come. Secondly, to listen to what my son was telling me. He named himself through this radiologist.

My son, in the womb, knew his purpose as well. He was meant to be named Arizona Blue. I have always believed that children pick their own names. It's up to the parents to listen closely to that inner guidance, or as in my case, the outer guidance of my radiologist.

✑ Experience: BE a voice

My grandmother began showing signs of Alzheimer's about four years before she died. The diagnosis of the disease was not a surprise, as the signs had been there for years. However, it was certainly a challenge to find the purpose of this particular disease, as it seems so devastating from almost every point of view.

Once diagnosed, and recognizing that safety was becoming an issue, my independent grandmother had to leave her home to move in with her daughters. It was a difficult thing for her to do, and she was, as one would guess, not happy about it. I remember her telling my mom that now that her house was sold, she didn't have a home – a common feeling amongst those who are stepping in between self-care and assisted living in some form. My Mom assured her that their homes were now hers. Having five daughters to depend on was certainly a relief after my grandpa died, but giving up her independence was difficult. Within a year or so of his death, the disease had progressed to a point where it was impossible for them to give her the quality of care she needed. They also found it increasing difficult to keep track of her. She was a wanderer. She just could not sit still for a moment, and so now safety had become a real issue.

The daughters made the decision to place her in an Assisted Living Care Center where she would get the 24-hour care that she needed. They chose an Assisted Living Facility with a secure Alzheimer's wing in Tucson, where my mother lived. The weather was beautiful in Arizona over the winter months, and she really loved the environment. My mom would visit her daily, facilitating activities for everyone. They would sing, play games, and do little brainteasers. It was a heart opening and heart breaking experience, all at the same time.

Even though Alzheimer's can be a devastating disease, I could see its purpose. It can be difficult to understand, but in some ways, Alzheimer's let me get to know my grandma on a deeper level. She was more present and in the moment than I had ever known her to be. You see, my grandma was an alcoholic my entire life, and most of her life as well, and Alzheimer's caused her to forget that, so she no longer drank. I know, it is ironic, isn't it? So you can understand how precious our time with her was! It was especially cool to get to see her so often because the previous 10 years I had lived out-of-state. During these times I really felt like we got to spend a lot of good quality time together. I had a baby at the time so my sons, my mom, Grandma and I would all sing nursery rhymes, eat ice cream, and just laugh and play ... it was a very special time together – the times I miss the most!

Spring came, the weather got warmer, and the decision was made for her to be in a cooler climate, where she could be outside more. The Arizona summers are extremely hot, and her being a wanderer was concerning because it was just too hot in Arizona for her to be outside. So she moved back to Utah, where she was originally from and where the majority of the family lived. They chose a new Assisted Living Center with a secure Alzheimer's wing, and she moved in April 2000. She lived there for eight months.

December 31, 2000 was a pretty normal day for me. I woke up around 6 a.m. and made breakfast for my family. Christmas had just passed, it was New Year's Eve, and my brother had come to visit for a few days. We were all in the kitchen just talking about the night's plans to celebrate "The Real Millennium." It was time to really celebrate the New Year, and we had decided to actually go out and have some fun instead of falling asleep watching the ball drop. I was excited to participate in the festivities, but I kept on having this heavy feeling creep in. I tried to ignore it, thinking it was just my fear of leaving my kids home or the drunk drivers on the road. As hard as I tried, it just wouldn't go away. Something was wrong, but I couldn't put my finger on it.

I finally told my family that I wasn't sure I wanted to go. Something just didn't feel right. I didn't know at the time that what I was feeling was a new purpose coming into my life, disguised as a painful and traumatic experience. It was then that the phone rang, and our lives changed forever.

My mother was calling, or at least that is what the caller ID said. It didn't sound like her, and I couldn't make out any of the words except "Grandma is dead." She was crying hysterically. I tried to get her to calm down as I truly could not understand what she was saying or why she was so upset. We had talked about Grandma dying several times and knew that once she died, she would be free from this terrible disease. In many ways, we thought it would be a relief when she finally did pass away, for everyone. So why was my Mother screaming uncontrollably? Well, after several minutes I found out why. My grandmother did die that morning, but not from Alzheimer's disease ... she died of hypothermia.

How? Why? Those were the questions that we asked in those initial hours, but no one knew the answers. Days and weeks later, information was released, and the pieces of the puzzle started to paint the picture. It felt as if we were in a nightmare as we learned of the last few hours leading up to Grandma's death. To our best knowledge, Grandma walked out of her "secure" Alzheimer's wing, and out of two other sets of doors without anyone noticing her. She walked 6/10 of a mile, in the middle of the night, in zero-degree weather with a silk nightgown on and bare feet. Her body was found 20 feet from the doorstep of someone's home. These are the facts as we know them. The how's and why's remain for many of the family members.

I also questioned the why, but soon turned my attention to a different question: "What could the purpose of this tragedy be?" There had to be a reason. I thought maybe I knew, but I wasn't quite sure yet. My grandmother deserved a peaceful death in her bed with her family surrounding her instead of wandering frightened, alone, in the dark, in the frigid night air. That is what my head said. My heart on the other hand, truly felt that there was a bigger picture to this story. I just didn't understand it yet, because I was in the human place of "Why?" I needed to move to a higher vibration in order to see the higher vision, and at that time, I simply wasn't there yet. So, I continued to ask the question: "What could the purpose of this tragedy be?"

Several days after my grandmother's death, I received my answer. My grandma came to me in Spirit form, and her presence was as clear to me as my hands are right now on my keyboard. She asked me – no, begged me to be HER voice. She wanted me to speak up for those patients who could not. People needed to know about the care facilities and their lack of focused attention, the ratio of caregiver to patients and the disregard for proper training. It was in that moment ... in her brief, but very powerful visit ... that I began to understand the bigger picture. Not only was I to find my purpose, but that of my grandmother's as well.

As I mentioned earlier, my grandmother was an alcoholic most of her life, and because she was not able to be present, she never truly felt like she was living her purpose, let alone had one. Yet now, in her death, she did. Her tragic ending would be the emotional voice and conduit that would bring about change. If I could be her VOICE, and I could share, then perhaps I could bring about awareness, and I could help my grandmother fulfill HER purpose while simultaneously fulfilling mine. I wanted people to know that in many cases, elder care living facilities are not managed well. I wanted to help educate people about the laws governing care facilities or the lack thereof and what really does take place behind the scenes.

I chose to honor Grandma by speaking to the media about the conditions that needed to be changed. I could no longer turn a blind eye to the elder care in our nation, and I didn't want anyone else to either. My family members and I wrote articles, interviewed patients and care givers and asked A LOT of questions. As we kept the conversation going, more people began to listen. Three of us went to the senate hearings in Washington DC on public policy and talked with our senators and our Governor and shared Grandma's story.

Most often the first response was empathy for the tragic way in which she died. That empathy inspired them to ask and to really want to see change come about. It was an amazing experience. And finally, because of my trip to DC, I became a board member of the Alzheimer's Association and a supporter of The Safe Return Program. If you are unfamiliar with this program, its purpose is to provide 24-hour nationwide emergency response service for individuals with Alzheimer's who wander away from their physical environment.

In sharing my grandmother's story, lives were not only spared but saved. OUR VOICES created public awareness which effectively created change in local laws. My grandmother is now the unspoken hero in the lives of many. They are the beneficiaries of better quality care, safer physical environments and higher standards for caregivers.

✂ Lesson:

My purpose in this experience was to listen clearly, take guided action and use MY voice. By taking action, speaking up and listening to my grandmother, WE made a difference. Through this experience, I learned what it meant to be authentic, and what it felt like to own my power. I understood for the first time that it was time to stop playing it safe. Up to this point, I was a stay-at-home mom and was quite happy doing that. However, something within me changed. The voice, the student and the teacher awoke in me. I was now ready to consciously live my purpose through teaching, speaking and sharing. Her death was the catalyst for me to release my fears and to put myself out there … in front of people.

I embraced my inner calling … to be who I really am and to use my VOICE. And to this day, I am still using my voice as a teacher, an author and an inspirational speaker. Grandma's story does not end here … I tell it quite often in my workshops and speaking engagements. She has been a beautiful teacher to me, and I stand in unending appreciation of all we have learned together.

My Mother's Heart

My Mother's heart is very warm
Her eyes extremely deep
They seem to hold a lifelong dream
Of which she cannot speak

She spends her time in solitude
It's always been that way
A kind and caring lonely soul
In many shades of gray.

I wish for her a happy life
And freedom from her pain
A sojourn filled with love and light
And shelter from the rain.

My Mother's heart is very warm
I know she'll find her way
Into the loving arms of God
Transcending shades of gray.

~ *This was written by my Mom, Solara Skye, three years before my Grandmother became free of her Alcoholism and Depression through the onset of Alzheimer's. It was three years later that she found her way home!*

How Do You Discover Your Purpose?

You discover your purpose by being present in the moment. Listening to your inner guidance. Paying attention to the messages you are receiving at any given time. Being aware of the feelings in your body when certain things awaken a desire within us. And being absolutely mindful of our thoughts. If purpose is within us, and you desire to discover consciously what your purpose is, then we must understand that spirit speaks to you in present moment. You cannot hear the message from spirit when thinking about the past or thinking about the future. Spirit speaks to you in present moment. It is a now experience.

Exercises to Discover Your Purpose

Here are some simple exercises to help you discover your purpose. These can be used daily, weekly, or any time you feel like something is shifting within you and you need more clarity or guidance.

☙ Automatic Writing /Journaling

This exercise can be done at any particular time when you are in need of clarity or guidance. As I have mentioned, your purpose is constantly changing as you change and grow and expand. So, this exercise may be helpful at any given time along your journey of life. Automatic writing will help you to be conscious of what is calling to you at this particular time in your life so that you can live intentionally and consciously.

Let's Begin:

- ☙ Create a space where you will not be interrupted for at least an hour. (No cell phone or computer either.)

- ☙ Have a couple of sheets of paper and a pen. No computer for this one, please.

❧ If you feel so guided, take a moment to ask the God of your understanding, your angels, spirit guides or any other spiritual deities for assistance in discovering your purpose. If this is new to you, you can ask Archangel Michael, who helps with Life Purpose and/or Archangel Uriel who helps with seeing the greater vision, for support and guidance.

❧ At the top of your paper, write: My purpose is …

❧ Now write anything and everything that comes into your awareness. Write without editing and without stopping. I call this stream of consciousness writing. It can be words, sentences, or phrases. It does not have to be complete sentences. As you write, observe your emotions and the feelings you have in your body.

❧ Continue writing until you either feel empty, it has been over a half hour, or you have a lot of emotion.

❧ Go through your list and mark the ones that brought up the most emotion in you. The ones that you could really feel in your heart. The ones that resonated with you. The ones that made you cry. The ones that gave you the chills. These messages, words and sentences are our purpose. So now that you have the words you will know what your purpose is … for now.

❧ Meditation

Meditation is a technique that is often used to receive guidance, focus energy and gain clarity. There are various forms of meditation and each person connects with meditation in a different way. Some focus on the breath, others an affirmation, others a vision, all to attain stillness. For when we are still, we are present, and when we are present, the purpose of the moment, day or our life can be revealed.

Let's Begin:

ↄ Create a space where you will not be interrupted for at least a half hour. No cell phone or computer. Nothing to distract you from the stillness. Make sure this is a safe and comfortable environment for you. You may want to have some sacred objects beside you, such as crystals, deities, incense, or a lit candle. It is your space, so create it to fit your energy and personality. I would suggest having a journal and a pen beside you for notes afterwards. A computer is fine, but have it off during the meditation.

ↄ Sit in a comfortable position. There are many suggested ways to sit. Many of them are also uncomfortable. Sit in whatever way is comfortable for you. On the floor or on a chair, even laying down is fine.

ↄ If you feel so guided, take a moment to ask the God of your understanding, your angels, spirit guides or any other spiritual deities for assistance in discovering your purpose. If this is new to you, you can ask Archangel Michael, who helps with Life Purpose and/or Archangel Uriel who helps with seeing the greater vision, for support and guidance.

ↄ Clear your mind. Release the tension from your body. Relax them both by focusing on your breath. Take a nice deep breath in, hold for 7 seconds, and out for 7 seconds. Let your breath become your focus.

ↄ Now just observe. Be a witness to your thoughts and feelings. Allow them to just drift in, and out, like clouds. With the thoughts coming in, you are now aware of what is always already there hidden by the thousands of other thoughts and feelings that you are feeling on a daily basis. The more aware you are, the quieter your mind becomes so that you can really be in touch with the quiet purpose within. So as you breathe in and out just let the everyday thoughts drift away, allowing yourself to go deeper within, reaching that stillness where spirit speaks to you, and reveals your purpose.

∽ When you feel complete, recharged, disconnected, take a few deep breaths, return back to your space and open your eyes.

∽ Now take a moment and write down anything that stays with you, anything you feel deep within, this is the guidance of your spirit. You can do this every day, keeping notes on what the messages are as you continue the meditation.

Please remember, with meditation, the more you do it the deeper you will go and the easier it will get. Practice, practice, practice and as that stillness comes to you and through you, with commitment and consistency, your greater purpose can and will be revealed.

Beliefs About Purpose

∽ **You don't get out of this life without serving your purpose.** *Everything happens for a reason, and when we say everything, it means everything. Therefore, purpose is being served in every situation and experience, whether we like it, believe that it is, or not.*

∽ **Purpose is not an "end of the rainbow" destination that we finally "get to."** *There is no destination to get to. Once born, we are all on our way to birth again, in the spirit world, or death as we call it here. Purpose is not complete until we die. You can't finish your purpose earlier than you finish your life experience. Purpose and life go hand in hand, together, moment by moment.*

∽ **Purpose is ever evolving and constant.** *You see, purpose changes as life changes. They go together like a beautiful marriage, as life grows and expands, so does our purpose. On any given day,* *you can be experiencing purpose in a completely different way than you did the week before.*

ᕩ **Purpose is a lifetime journey.** *Purpose does not end. Even when this physical journey ends and we go back into spirit, we are still purposeful. We are just not living physical beings.*

ᕩ **Purpose is not some grandiose thing that only the successful people experience.** *Purpose happens. Regardless of what our perception of someone's life experience is, it is their purpose. Different areas of the world experience life differently. Who are we to judge that because someone has less money or lives in a tent that they are not living their purpose? Every one, in every way, is serving their purpose. Even if it is seemingly difficult to look at.*

ᕩ **Purpose is innate.** *It is who we are, who we are meant to be, at any given time. You can't run away from what is within you! You are spirit embodied, and so too is your purpose, dwelling within.*

My Discovery

People experience life in a variety of ways, and none of those ways are right or wrong, just different. I tend to look at my life experiences as opportunities to expand and learn. Oftentimes, I am then guided to share and teach from these experiences as well. Throughout the years, by learning to stay present and seeing the broader picture of the events around me, I have discovered that for ME, in this journey of life, my purpose is to BE. It is to experience life. To live it to its fullest in the present moment. I believe that if I am in the present moment, I can BE love. I am love! You are love! We are love! Bottom line, my purpose is to BE LOVE, always and in all ways.

I have expressed that love in a variety of ways: Joy, excitement, passion, hope, laughter, etc. Sometimes it has been more of a cry for love instead of an expression of love. I have expressed that cry for love in a variety of ways, too: Fear, sadness, depression, guilt, shame, illness, etc. Each and every one of these expressions has been a part of my purpose, whether I knew it at the time or not. Love runs through all of the experiences in my life, in some form. Isn't that exciting to know?

As you read this book, I believe that these stories will not only inspire you but will help you to see that purpose lies in every life experience, and hopefully help you to recognize the purpose living in your life right now. So please, continue the journey, and allow the purpose of this book to express itself to you through the stories of my friends, students, clients and colleagues.

This book is dedicated to each and every spirit that has crossed my path and helped me live my purpose, knowingly or unknowingly. I am forever grateful.

~ Sunny Dawn Johnston

The purpose of life
is a life of purpose.

~ ROBERT BYRNE

Nancy Newman

NANCY A NEWMAN is a licensed Heal Your Life® Coach, Workshop Facilitator and Teacher with a private practice, Mindful Wellness, in Spokane, WA. She is also an author and speaker empowering people world-wide to live their authentic lives by sharing her personal stories, facilitating workshops and teaching the tools for healing, loving yourself and discovering the peace within.

Nancy is also a registered Master Toe Reader, Reiki Master and Reflexologist. She enjoys traveling to Portland, OR to spend time with her son, daughter-in-law and grandbabies, London Ava and Camden Wilson.

nancy@toelady.com
www.toelady.com

Get On With It!

You've Got the Gift

The stranger sat on the edge of the podium in front of me, flicking her teeth with a toothpick. "You've got the gift, don't you?" she said while eyeing me disdainfully. "Yes," I shyly replied, becoming increasingly uncomfortable. "Then why aren't you using it?" Feeling like a naughty schoolgirl, I found myself stuttering and stammering lame excuses in response: "Well, I'm searching for my path," or "You see, I grew up in Texas where I was ridiculed for it," and, and, and, and ... but she wasn't having any part of it.

While her eyes bored into mine causing me to squirm under her gaze, she finished: "Excuses. Not reasons, excuses. **GET ON WITH IT.**"

Who **was** this woman?

We were on the noon break of an all-day workshop with Dr. Brian Weiss before the main *I Can Do It!* Conference in Las Vegas. I was reading a book, and hadn't noticed this woman in front of me until she began speaking. When she finished lecturing me, I watched her sit down on the front row, about two seats to the side of me, just as Dr. Weiss was beginning to speak again for the afternoon session.

By the first break I had regained my composure, and I immediately stood up and turned to say something to her, but she was not sitting in her chair. Someone else was sitting there. I had not seen any movement out of my peripheral vision or heard anyone moving, nor did I hear the heavy conference room doors opening and closing if someone had left and someone else came in.

Where could the mystery woman be? More importantly: Who was she?

I asked the lady who was now sitting in that chair and the other people sitting next to me, "Where is the woman who was sitting there after lunch?" They all agreed that no one else had been there, the current seat occupant had been sitting in that seat all day. It wasn't until later I realized I had had my first known contact from a non-physical entity with a message from the Universe. Whether she was a guide or an angel or even a spirit, her message was not lost on me. GET ON WITH IT!

Don't Confuse the Path with the Destination

 Your purpose in life is to find your purpose and give your whole heart and soul to it.

~ BUDDHA

How many of us are feeling that restless stirring, the "knowing" that there is something calling to us, something we're supposed to be doing, but we're not sure exactly what it is? That "something" is our Soul, stirring us to action, stirring us to fulfill our purpose.

As I approached my sixth decade, I was experiencing that limbo in which so many find themselves. I knew there was a reason for my being on earth, but thinking of my *SOUL PURPOSE* just seemed so spiritual, so intense, I believed there had to be more to it than "just" the sum of my life! I began reading every spiritual self-help book I could find, going to every conference, workshop and class I could manage, getting one certification after another, always seeking the elusive "purpose" and never quite finding the path to that purpose. Or so I thought.

 If you can see your path laid out in front of you step by step, you know it's not your path. Your own path you make with every step you take. That's why it's your path.

~ JOSEPH CAMPBELL

Your overall destined purpose is to be happy, and to be the very best YOU that you can be in service to others! That's it. While the path to fulfill our purpose is unique for everyone, our purpose is the same: Be happy, and be the very best YOU that you can be in service to others.

At different times in our lives, we walk different parts of the path to this purpose. For example, for a lot of women, being the very best mother they can be occupies the first part of their adult lives. Then as their life evolves, so does the path to their purpose. But everything we experience is part of that path to our purpose. Don't confuse the path with the destination! We will be walking this path our whole life, and each section will contribute to our purpose.

They Don't Build Lighthouses on Sandy Beaches

A few months after my encounter with the non-physical entity in Las Vegas, I went to another national conference, *Celebrate Your Life,* in Scottsdale, Arizona. The scheduled speaker for the all-day workshop on the last day had to withdraw unexpectedly, so spiritual teacher Michael Tamura filled in. I was not familiar with Michael at that time, but I accepted that there was a reason I needed to be in his workshop.

As the seats in the workshop were filling up, I suddenly realized that there was a man sitting about two seats down from me. The only access to that seat was to cross in front of me, but I didn't recall anyone doing that. We nodded and exchanged pleasantries.

After lunch, I suddenly realized that he was again sitting about two seats down from me, and he was just staring at me with a stern look of disapproval. I got the feeling that he was like my strictest teacher in High School, Mrs. Lowenstein, and I had somehow done something wrong. I remember feeling like I had forgotten my homework, or I was in trouble somehow.

He was asking me what I "did," and I told him I was searching for my purpose. I knew I was a writer, teacher and healer, but I didn't know how that fit together as my "purpose." I shared that I lived in a very conservative small town where the majority of people did not share my beliefs. I was sure that I needed to be somewhere more accepting of me and my beliefs. I added that I would love to move back to Scottsdale where I could be surrounded with like-minded people.

The exact instant I uttered those words, the sound of conversation in the room suddenly receded into the background, and it seemed as if a large bubble with a blurry boundary had surrounded us, separating us from the room. His look seemed to pierce straight into my Soul as he said, "They don't build lighthouses on sandy beaches, do they?"

For me, it was a moment of crystal clarity. I realized in that instant that it was my choice whether or not to move back to Scottsdale, and "play" with like-minded people on the "sandy beach," or to remain in Spokane and be a "light" on the rocky shore for those "lost in an angry sea." Was I going to preach to the choir, or was I going to do the real work? That was my purpose, to be a lighthouse and a beacon of hope for others. With an intense, penetrating look, he said sternly: "**GET ON WITH IT**."

Immediately, the blurry boundary dissolved, the sound of conversation resumed, and the strange man next to me was chatting away as if nothing extraordinary had just happened. I realized that I had just had my second encounter with a non-physical entity.

After that, I received many messages from psychics which also included the phrase, "Get on with it." But what was I supposed to "get on" with? If my purpose was to be a lighthouse, just how was I supposed to do that? I was still searching because I believed it had to be something more than being "just" a writer, teacher and healer.

Other Messengers Sent by Spirit

At that same conference in Scottsdale, I was introduced to Toe Reading. I was amazed at the accuracy of the readings from these toe readers. I sampled toe readings twice more at different conferences before deciding to attend a workshop with the originator of Toe Reading, KC Miller. I wanted to see if perhaps THIS was what I was supposed to "get on" with.

While KC was talking, she was wandering around the audience, looking at toes and making observations as she spoke. She initially walked past me sitting in my aisle seat, then paused, backed up and looked directly at me with an emphatic point of her index finger and said: "What if *YOU* were the messenger sent by Spirit to help this Soul back on its path?" Whoa. I felt as if I had been riveted back into my seat by the force of those words, and that the Universe was speaking directly to me, into my very soul.

The words in her message were not only to help me get on my path, but also to help me realize that the two non-physical entities were messengers sent by Spirit, and that KC Miller was herself a messenger sent by Spirit.

After studying for nearly two years at the Southwest Institute of Healing Arts in Tempe, Arizona, I received the designation of Master Toe Reader. I thought I had found my path, and I was on my way. Well, I was, but not as I expected.

I subsequently studied with Dr. Patricia Crane and Rick Nichols with Heart Inspired Presentations™ receiving my license from Heal Your Life® to teach Louise Hay principles. A few months after that, I received my license to do one-on-one life coaching for Heal Your Life®. I thought I had found the final piece for "my purpose." But again, my path was to take another turn.

I had really bonded with one of the other students at my Heal Your Life® training, Lisa Hardwick, who invited me to do a chapter in a multi-author book, *Beyond Beautiful*. What a dream! I had wanted to be a published author since I was eight years old. I began editing for the publisher for that and subsequent books, then after another year, Lisa and I began our own publishing company, Visionary Insight Press.

So now I had the pieces to my puzzle: I was a writer (with Visionary Insight Press), a teacher (as a HYL coach) and a healer (as a toe reader). Just as I had imagined all along: A writer, a teacher and a healer! With all the pieces in place, I was now "getting on with it," or so I thought. There was just one little hitch: I was still working a full-time job with a law firm and could only do my "purpose" at night and on the weekends.

Soon, the Universe sent another messenger. A serious disagreement with one of the partners at my law firm resulted in my being asked to leave my position as a paralegal. My immediate feeling was one of relief. NOW I would have the freedom to "get on with it" by living my heart's desire and doing what gives me joy every day. I am so grateful for the angry partner, who I now realize was just another messenger sent by Spirit!

In the Being Comes the Doing

 There is no greater gift you can receive than to honor your calling. It's why you were born. And how you become most truly alive.

~ OPRAH WINFREY

What I have now discovered is that in doing my writing, my coaching, my toe reading, my publishing, I am actually drawing on my *entire* life's experiences! Everything I have experienced, good and bad, I am able to utilize in these areas to be of service to Spirit and others. Every thread in the tapestry of my life to this point was necessary to "get on with it" and do my purpose! Nothing was a waste of time, everything had meaning and purpose. I had been on my path and fulfilling my purpose all along. I had just been confusing my path with the destination.

Even when we are on our path, and feel we've found our purpose, we will still find ourselves constantly evolving, refining our "purpose." I don't think that any of us ever get "there." When we reach our final destination, it's time to leave the planet! So when we get "there," we will discover that there is another "there" just ahead!

You don't need to suffer or struggle to find your purpose. Don't concern yourself with finding the perfect well-paying career, or quitting your job, or starting a new one. Instead, just follow your heart, your natural talents and desires which will naturally bring joy to you and others.

The purpose of your life is to serve in a way that brings great joy to yourself and others. Don't worry about finding your purpose. Instead, focus upon serving a purpose, and then your purpose will serve you.

~ DOREEN VIRTUE

People will be drawn to you by who *YOU* are, not by any certifications or initials after your name. Your life purpose doesn't need to be specifically identified or defined. There is no perfect time to begin. You will never be "there." There is no final destination. Your life purpose is an ever-changing, evolving process, not a simple category. Just be yourself, and in the being comes the doing.

What Are You Waiting For?

Seriously, what are you doing to get on the path to happiness which will lead to your Soul purpose? What are you waiting for? A knock on the door from Opportunity? A messenger from Spirit? Allow me to be your messenger, and the message is pretty straightforward: Eliminate from your life those things, persons and situations which do not bring you joy and happiness; bring into your life those things which do!

 I believe our Soul Purpose is to be happy and to strive for our full potential using our gifts and abilities in service to others.

~ NANCY NEWMAN

Sometimes it is hard to identify exactly what our gifts and abilities are. Perhaps we just take them for granted and think everyone has this or can do that. Perhaps we have accepted as our truth what others believe are our gifts and abilities (or lack thereof), and how we "should" be happy!

So first of all, ask yourself, "Am I happy? Am I joyful?" If not, the process to identify what in your life is making you unhappy should be relatively easy. If you cannot eliminate the source of your unhappiness, you can absolutely change the way you think about it by reframing it.

Next, ask yourself: "What did I enjoy doing as a child? What did I want to be when I 'grew up'?" These childhood dreams often illuminate our true, hidden gifts and abilities.

What do you enjoy doing in your spare time? What is something you do that makes the time seem to stand still or melt away? What do you feel you are here to give to others?

Can you make your living doing that "thing" you so enjoy? Don't just automatically say no! As Joseph Campbell says, "When you follow your bliss, the Universe will open doors where before there were only walls." Think about what it is you can do right now to be one step closer to doing what you love. Is it classes to refine your skill or knowledge? Investigating the steps to open a business? Interviewing others who have taken the path you want to follow?

As you start to align your vibrations from that which does not bring happiness to a vibration of that which does, you will automatically start to see possibilities in your life to bring that joy and happiness to others!

Still your mind, allow your Soul to speak. The answer is inside you!

And the day came when the risk to remain tight in a bud was more painful than the risk it took to blossom.

~ ANAIS NIN

What are you waiting for? Take a risk! Do whatever it takes for your Soul to blossom. The path to happiness and joy will lead you to your Soul purpose. GET ON WITH IT!

Dedicated to the messengers in my life, past, present and future, who have appeared at the precise moment I was ready for their message; and to Spirit for guiding me to become a messenger to help Souls back on their paths.

I want to acknowledge and thank everyone who has been a part of my life's journey. You have all been my teachers who have knowingly and unknowingly helped me put Humpty Dumpty back together again so I can be a messenger and a humble servant to those in need. My Soul sings when I am serving Spirit!

~ Nancy Newman

Paula Obeid

PAULA OBEID had a spiritual awakening in 2010 while taking a nine-month Mind, Body & Soul certification with her mentor, Sunny Dawn Johnston. Her life purpose was revealed, and she shifted to a service-oriented career which supports individuals as they move into living their authentic lives. Paula has studied with other spiritual teachers but was privileged to spend a week in a private setting with Louise Hay and Cheryl Richardson. Paula loves facilitating events as executive founder of the Non-Profit Heart-Centered Endeavors which empowers individuals by finding the self-love within themselves while pursuing their dreams.

Heartcentered1111@gmail.com
www.heartcenteredendeavors.com

❧ Why Wasn't I Told This Before?

Who is born knowing what their life purpose is? Many spend a lifetime searching for their life purpose, only to find that it was within us the whole time. At least, that is what I discovered for myself. In fact, most of my life I was not even consciously searching for purpose. I guess you could say I didn't even know I was lost.

What I discovered was so simple that I had to wonder "why wasn't I told this before?" I finally realized that I was not lost and that my soul was born knowing my life purpose, but I just had to slow down and learn how to listen.

Life purpose is about following your dreams, and sometimes just about getting your ego out of the way and letting a dream unfold. This past year for me has been a life of what dreams are made of, but if you ask any of my close friends, the life I live was never my dream. I am one year shy of my 50th birthday, and I feel that I am just starting to step into my life purpose. How does a 49-year-old software engineer shift careers going from engineering to opening a foundation that teaches classes about intuition and finding the gratitude in life? Simplest answer is: Letting go and learning to listen to spirit. I feel that the most exciting, rewarding years of my life are ahead of me.

For 20 years I was living the life of an analytical engineer – always in my head! I was president of an engineering company that had many technology advances, one of which Software Development Magazine recognized the company's collaborative development of SysML as the most innovative technology of 2006. Prior to co-founding the engineering firm with my husband, I was the Process Group Lead in the Aerospace Division of Honeywell. While at Honeywell, I helped develop and deploy Software Six Sigma to Software Engineers and was the Honeywell Representative in industry organizations like SAE, helping to create standards for deliverable software and quality. I had a very satisfying career and thought that engineering was what I would do until I retired.

My life could have been considered a life of "good enough." My forties were the saddest but happiest years of my life. I was widowed when I was 40 and lost my mother to cancer six years later. Although my life was marred with many more "challenges" during this period of my life, I was primarily happy.

I believe that we have a choice at various points in our life on how we react or feel about an event in our life. I also have come to believe that we all have a life plan, "soul contract", that we chose before we were born. Although we have a "soul contract," free will gives us the opportunity to change our life at various choice points in our lives. As we encounter "challenges" in our life, we can choose love or fear.

Discerning your life purpose is going to be about walking through your fears and trusting you will be supported by the universe. Even when we know that something good is going to happen, we often self-sabotage. By choosing love, especially self-love, we can move forward into our purpose. We have the capability to continue to live a life of "good enough," or we can decide at any time that we can live a life of dreams. The choice is ours.

We are born into a world that tries to tell us who we are and what we should be from the day we are born. The medical profession tells our parents what weight or height we as babies should be at three months, nine months and a year. Our parents doing the best they can to start to condition us from infancy to conform to what society dictates we should be. As we grow, our trusted parents, family, friends and teachers start to help re-program us to forget who we are and what our soul chose as our life purpose. Society and the media then continue to persuade us as to what we should be doing with our life.

Socially-imposed limitations such as age, education, economics and family conditions will not hold us back from living our purpose and dreams. Our thoughts which are limited by external messages can hold us back from our dreams, since if we think something cannot happen, it won't. Would you ever squash a child's dream by attaching a bunch of doubts to their dream? You also deserve the same support you offer to others, so find a gentle supportive voice to nurture your dreams. We get enough strong messages from external sources that are affecting what we think we should be doing with our life. Messages that tell us to be the good child, the good student, the good worker, the good partner and the good parent! Messages that don't include being loving to yourself. I believe our soul's journey in this lifetime is to re-discover self-love and what our soul chose as a life purpose.

You can head to any bookstore and find row after row of books trying to teach us self-love. Self-love is so important that most of us dedicate a good portion of our life journey on this subject. Part of this self-discovery opens us up to see how extraordinary we are and guides us to our life purpose. Self-love allows our soul to ignore the external sources that keep influencing us when our soul was born knowing what our life purpose was the whole time. So if you are trying to attain your life purpose, one path is for it to be revealed as you work on your self-love journey.

External sources also plant the seeds of vicious soundtracks that hold us back in our life and put limits on what we can conceive. The cruelest of these soundtracks is self-judgment. Sometimes we view ourselves as not good enough to live our dreams, and that others around us know more, communicate better, have more talent, or are more deserving than us to live their purpose and dreams.

Internal soundtracks that are very critical of ourselves are only a distraction from discovering what we really want to do with our life. We would never talk to our child or any child the way we do to ourselves. If we start to use a loving tone when we talk to our inner child, we can start to change those critical soundtracks that hold us back. If we stop listening to those external messages and go internal, we could tap into our life purpose which our soul knows and chose without limitations. How great a feeling is it to tap into our truth?

Listen internally, your soul will guide you and help you remember why you are here. Your soul does not have the limitations of your mind and the world. Our job is to learn to trust. I know that is hard for many like me who come from abusive childhoods or have had dysfunctional relationships. The hardest part is trusting ourselves which is another reason the key to discerning your life purpose is to embark on a journey of self-love.

I also know that sometimes when I would listen internally, I was fearful since the messages were not what I wanted to hear and were inconvenient. But I continued to listen internally and trust my intuition. More importantly, I started acting on what spirit was saying internally and moving forward in confidence knowing that I would be supported. This was new for me since I didn't trust my intuition. I had strong soundtracks that others were intuitive but not me. Three years ago, I might have even told you that I am not sure if I believed that anyone was intuitive. I would have told you I was good at reading a person's character and had good logic. After all, I was the analytical engineer. I always thought that others had good intuition but not me, so I rarely turned internally for guidance.

Do you recognize similar soundtracks? I know that taking Sunny's nine-month Mind, Body and Soul Certification after my mother transitioned from cancer helped me start to go internally and listen. I started to realize I was intuitive and to find the trust in my internal guidance. I am grateful for Sunny's Sunlight Alliance Healing Center and the affiliated community and eternal friendships which were supportive in my journey of self-love. I suggest finding a like-minded community or individual to support you as you embark on your journey.

I believe that there is a shift of consciousness taking place on the planet. I believe that many individuals born during this time have "soul contracts" with a purpose to help humanity get to a more heart-centered world. We are moving toward a more intuitive conscious world and awakening spiritually. So if you have not been able to tune into your inner voice in the past, I suspect that you will now be able to hear the inner voice which will assist discerning your purpose.

During the last two years, I have been quickly evolving spiritually, as I suspect many are. I have always been a loving, compassionate person and ME at the core. But in the last two years, many of my belief systems have changed. I quickly discovered life had other plans for me than my engineering path. I now embrace my spiritual side and found a purpose in helping raise the vibration of this planet.

In fact, I believe that all of us have the same purpose to discover self-love and joyously raise the vibration of this planet. I say joyously since if we are all doing things that make us happy, we are raising the vibration of the planet. How we each help raise the vibration is uniquely our journey and, therefore, the variance in each of our paths and purposes. Remember we are all connected, and each of our contributions to raising the vibration is important. Don't judge your contribution to be insignificant or less than another since that is just another critical soundtrack from external sources.

Remember we were born knowing our life purpose and need to trust that we have everything within us to support us achieving our purpose. We can stop searching outside of us for what we were born to achieve. By dropping all boundaries imposed by external sources, you can live your purpose and live a limitless life embracing all that you can conceive. Trust that the universe will support your dreams when you are living your soul's purpose. I know my journey this past year of standing in my purpose has been astonishing and rewarding.

Let me be the one to tell you that finding your life purpose is easy. Your purpose has been within you since the day you were born. Your mission is to find your unique path to continue your journey of self-love while raising the vibration of this planet as you live the joyous life of your dreams! I am off to speculate "why wasn't I told this before."

Dedicated to my friends and family who have supported and loved me unconditionally on my journey of self-love. Especially my beloved children, Sarah and Adam, who have shown me that "While we try to teach our children all about life, our children teach us what life is all about. – Anonymous."

I want to express infinite love and gratitude to my family and friends who have supported and loved me unconditionally. I also want to express gratitude for family and friends no longer in my life, since you have been my greatest teachers. Each and every one of you has shown up in my life perfectly to support my soul's growth. My wish for everyone is that we all awaken to discover a future of love and limitless potential. I don't have the space to acknowledge each and every one of you by name since I am so blessed to have so many wonderful souls in my life journey. Finally, I would like to thank Sunny Dawn Johnston and her Sunlight Alliance Team since they have touched my life and many others as we awaken to self-love and our life purposes.

~ Paula Obeid

Shanda Bisanz

SHANDA BISANZ is a certified Mind, Body and Spirit Practitioner, Workshop Facilitator, and Spiritual Counselor who specializes in coaching those who wish to discover their life's purpose and awaken to their divine mission.

She is also the Founder of Spiritual Writers Network, a networking website where writers can connect with one another, share their writing, and find resources and opportunities with other like-minded individuals within the spiritual community.

Shanda resides in Tampa Bay, Florida. She enjoys traveling, writing, and spending time at the beach.

shanda@spiritualwritersnetwork.com
www.spiritualwritersnetwork.com
www.shandabisanz.com

Searching for Purpose

 If you can't figure out your purpose, figure out
your passion. For your passion will lead you right
into your purpose.

~ BISHOP T.D. JAKES

As far back as I can remember, I have been searching for a life of
purpose and meaning. I always believed I was destined to do something amazing with my life, I just hadn't found out yet what that was. I
firmly believed I was just passing time working in various occupations
until my chosen path would magically appear before me.

Being the free spirit that I am, I have always enjoyed traveling and
seeing new places. In my twenties, I moved frequently trying to find a
place where I felt settled, and I could make my home. As a bartender by
trade, this vocation offered me that freedom as there was always a bar
in every town willing to let me pour drinks for their devoted regulars.

Finding a bartending job was something that had always come easy to
me, and since I started when I was just a teenager, I had racked up skills
and experience. Doors always seemed to open, and I would just happen
to find myself in the right place at the right time – almost as if it was
meant to be. The money was good for the hours I worked, and I wasn't

stuck behind a desk eight hours a day, so it seemed a perfect fit for me. Still, I knew there was something greater out there just waiting for me.

I have always been a spiritual person, but over time I struggled with the lifestyle of a bartender and found that if I didn't keep my mind busy, the temptation of spending too much time in that environment would get the best of me. Late nights would turn into lazy mornings, and I would go in and out of focusing on my spiritual work. As a result, by my late twenties, I found myself trying to break away from bartending, but I could never quite find the right niche.

I dabbled in many things trying to find a new profession that suited me. I tried various sales positions but was never quite aggressive enough to close the deal. I signed up for several pyramid schemes, but those always seemed to promise more than they delivered. I spent several months going to school to be an esthetician, because my sister was making a lot of money at it; but after I earned my license, I realized I didn't like the skincare field. I had a friend who was making a great living as a Realtor, so I went to school to obtain my real estate license, and ultimately decided that also was not a fit for me.

I was trying to do what had made others successful, in hopes that I would find the same success. I didn't realize I was trying to live someone else's dream, and I wasn't following where my own bliss led me. So I went back to my old faithful, bartending, always there to welcome me with open arms. It was almost too easy.

By my thirties, I had been bartending for over ten years, and I was growing anxious to find my real life purpose. Bartending was no longer fulfilling, and I found myself dreading going to work each day in a career that was not satisfying. I started to feel as if the customers were sucking the life and energy right out of me with their many problems. Then to make matters worse, I kept finding myself in unwanted bar management positions. I was not looking to be the boss, and I had no need for the extra responsibility, I simply wanted to work my bartending shifts and be free to use my spare time to find that purpose I knew was just right around the corner.

Somehow though, each bar I worked at kept giving me more and more responsibility, and before I knew it, I was both bartending and running the bar, which meant even more hours in that dreadful place, much to my dismay. *So be it*, I finally surrendered. I figured at least that way I could write my own schedule, so I could work on what brought me joy in my spare time and be ready when fate came knocking.

Through all the moves and job changes, and my desire to find my purpose, I always continued my spiritual studies. I devoured any and all metaphysical books that I could get my hands on, but mostly I loved learning about angels. I discovered early on in my spiritual journey how blessed life can be when you call on the angels to guide you in any situation. I also realized that I enjoyed teaching others about angels. This brought me pleasure, and I admired teachers like Doreen Virtue and Sunny Dawn Johnston for being able to write and teach the world about the miraculous power of working with angels.

Hmm...maybe this is my calling? I couldn't help but wonder.

Continuing my spiritual studies, I stumbled upon another genre that is dear to my heart, the Law of Attraction. Once I read *The Secret* and learned about this theory, I started reading any and all books of its kind. Applying the principles in the Law of Attraction has completely changed my life for the better, and I found myself no longer struggling for abundance and prosperity. I manifested a miraculous life for myself using these concepts. Before long I had a beach-front home in Florida, owned the convertible I always wanted, attracted a fulfilling and loving relationship, and many money channels also started to flow to me. Doors began opening for me, and I found myself attracting amazing opportunities and experiences into my life. I can honestly say I live a joyous and blessed life.

I felt guided to share this information with the world, so in my spare time, I studied under Dr. Joe Vitale and the Global Sciences Foundation and became a certified Law of Attraction Practitioner. When I wasn't working in the bar, I spent my time writing a book which breaks down the basic concepts of the Law of Attraction to teach others how to manifest their best life by following seven simple steps. I also started a website, blog, and Facebook page to share positive messages of inspiration and love with the world. This seemed to bring me some fulfillment while still working at the bar (*sigh*), and still searching for my purpose ...

By my mid-thirties this waiting was really starting to wear on me. I just knew I should be working in my desired field and living my purpose, but I couldn't figure out what that purpose was. Every time I would find myself in the presence of a psychic, astrologer, or visionary, I would ask them what my purpose was, but to my dismay, I never seemed to get a straight answer. I would do angel card readings to try to find my purpose, but I always seemed to get the same message: Focus on service and your purpose will serve you.

Oh how frustrating! What does that mean? I only serve drinks, and I give good service, but why should I focus on serving drinks?

The answer was there all along, but I didn't see it.

In April of 2012, I was fortunate enough to attend one of Sunny Dawn Johnston's healing retreats in Sedona, Arizona. This was a wonderful experience, and I would strongly recommend it to anyone who feels guided to attend one of her retreats. While at the retreat, I received a reading from one of Sunny's staff members, Amy Richmond. I remember feeling so anxious about my reading because I knew exactly what I was going to ask. I couldn't wait for her to tell me what my life purpose was, and I was just sure that she would know. Amy was giving a lengthy reading to the person before me, and I was getting antsy. I felt I was destined for something greater, and she was going to tell me exactly what it was! I could hardly sit still.

Finally, it was my turn to sit and talk with Amy. She asked me if I had a specific question or concern. With unwavering certainty I announced, "Yes, I am unfulfilled in my line of work, and I really want to start working on my life purpose."

Probably even before she realized she had done it, she started chuckling at my reply. I couldn't believe it! *Why is she laughing at me? Certainly that was a good question.* She must have seen the look of confusion on my face because she pulled herself together and replied, "My dear, don't you think you have been working on your life purpose your whole life?"

Ahhhhhhhh.

I sat in silence as the words sank in. It was in that moment that I finally realized that I *had* been working on my life purpose my entire life. From my childhood experiences, through my troubled teens, to my free-spirited twenties; every decision and every incident in my life had made me the very person sitting in that chair at that moment. All my experiences, both good and bad, and all the knowledge I acquired along the way, made me a soul packed full of useful information. Experiences and information that I could share with the world! Still, I couldn't help but wonder, *why am I still working in a bar?*

As we were leaving the retreat, several of us were hesitant to return back to our everyday lives. We were all vibrating on such a high level from all the spiritual healing work we had done over the past several days. Many of us feared that going back to our jobs and our family and friends might somehow bring down our vibration. As a spiritual teacher who is guided by Spirit, Sunny must have sensed this, because she left us with this final thought before departing: *Do not let anyone bring down your vibration. Instead, bring their vibration up!*

So that is precisely what I set out to do. Upon returning home I remembered to ground myself before I went to work each day, and I asked Archangel Michael to protect me and to repel any negativity. I decided to radiate love to everyone with whom I crossed paths and not let anyone bring down my spirit. Well, can you imagine what happened? I immediately started to attract people into my life who were interested in what I had to offer. In the very bar that had brought me such misery, I found there were so many souls in need of my help and knowledge.

People started to ask me where I had gone for a week and what I did while I was there. As I started to explain, some of the patrons showed interest and started opening up to me. Acting on my promise to radiate love, I started working with them. Before you knew it, I was a go-to person for many of the lost souls out there. It turns out, those people needed me and that felt good. Finally, it wasn't a chore to go to work. In addition, I found so many like-minded souls who were also into spirituality with whom I just hadn't brought the subject up before. I stopped looking at what I did for a living as useless and unfulfilling and realized that I am not just a bartender, I am a lightworker shining light in a dark place.

It seems as if there is a shift occurring, and more and more the universe is in need of lightworkers. Lightworkers can be found everywhere, in every field and in every community. Those of us who were put on this earth to shine our light on others may find ourselves in a variety of occupations. I used to think the lightworkers and spiritual people of the world were gathered together in a sort of group. But if that were the case, then who would do God's work and help others in need?

In hindsight, I have learned that all the while I was out searching for my purpose, I was actually living my purpose all along. There is a reason why all those bartending jobs came easy to me, and I always found myself pulled back into that trade. Those people needed me to do more than serve their drinks. They need me to listen, to give them advice, to pray for them, to send them healing love and light, and to raise *their* vibration. My current occupation brings me the people I am aligned to work with, and I now know that does not mean my place of employment has to define my life purpose. It is what you do with what you are given that truly matters.

Now my focus is on teaching others how to enrich their lives through the help of the angels and the miraculous power of the Law of Attraction. Together, this is a strong combination for both healing and manifesting. When someone is open to my knowledge, I find myself teaching them how to see the positive side of any situation, and how to keep their thoughts positive with the use of daily affirmations. I guide others how to use the manifesting concepts of the Law of Attraction which I talk about in my book.

I will often advise people which angel to call upon to help with their current situation, which colors and gemstones are associated with that angel, an invocation to use to connect to a particular angel, and how to communicate with and receive messages from the angels. I find passion and great joy in teaching others about angels and the Law of Attraction, and it's very rewarding to watch miraculous occurrences unfold in the lives of others.

Lightworkers can be found everywhere, and we are in high demand. We are here to raise the world's vibration through love, light, and inspiration. Although I still feel as though I am intended for something greater than the line of work I am currently in, for now, I realize I am exactly where I am meant to be in this moment, and I am ultimately the creator of my destiny. I am no longer looking for my purpose, because I now know, I AM living my purpose.

Dedicated to all who are searching for a purpose. May you acknowledge and trust your divine gifts within and become a beacon of light wherever you may stand. Shine on!

With love and gratitude to Sunny Dawn Johnston, who has become a valued teacher and mentor along my spiritual path. To Anthony for always believing in me and supporting my journey. With special thanks to my mother, Diana, for teaching me independence and giving me the strength and freedom to explore who I truly am and find my own way in this world. Each of you have given me the wings to make all of my dreams come true.

~ Shanda Bisanz

When you dance, your purpose is not to get to a certain place on the floor. It's to enjoy each step along the way.

~ WAYNE DYER

Kim Richardson

KIM RICHARDSON is a teacher, motivational speaker, coach, and mentor who, through sharing her own personal experiences, helps empower individuals to transform their lives. Kim fills her spare time spreading her passion for scuba diving by helping teach others the wonders of our water friends and the marvels of the sea.

Kim resides in Phoenix, Arizona where she enjoys the warm weather and sunshine while spreading her love with her friends and family. Her passion for spreading love, helping all to heal, forgive and grow while teaching compassion inspire all who know her.

Kim.richardson444@yahoo.com

❦ Discovering and Living My Life Purpose

How do you discover your life purpose? I believe the answer is simple but in the form of another question: What brings you the most joy?

When I was a senior in high school, I went to cosmetology school. I knew when I graduated, my life's purpose was to teach. I worked in a salon for a year to gain some experience and then went back to obtain my cosmetology instructor's license. This new world was rewarding for me. The joy I felt every day watching students grow and learn was revealing for me with what they taught me. As a result, every day I grew, learning so much from everyone that joined my journey. At the time I only knew that I wanted to change the industry. Who knew at that time it would lead to much more? Teaching has brought me to discover my purpose.

While I was teaching in a cosmetology school, I continued working at a salon because of my love for my clients. I loved connecting with people and being such an important part of their lives. Little did they know how much they were helping me to grow. I enjoyed listening, helping, guiding and most importantly making them feel great about themselves. I have learned to accept people for who they are rather than trying to change them or judge them. I have learned compassion for their lives and their journeys. I feel my greatest sense of accomplishment is when I see a "light bulb" moment in a student's, stylist's or another teacher's eyes. It's so rewarding to be able to pass on your knowledge and experience and see someone's life change as a result of that knowledge that you shared.

Now I realize this journey of my life was merely the angels' preparation for my true purpose. As time has passed, I have grown on my spiritual path. I now realize my true purpose. I would have never discovered it without some difficult lessons and hard work over the past years. There is always a reason for everything in our life, even if we may not understand it at the moment it happens. There is a lesson and a gift with every moment in our life; we just need to be open to seeing them.

During my eighteen years in the cosmetology industry, I have worked in many facets of the industry. Today I am managing a cosmetology school, the largest I have ever managed. With it comes many challenges. Cultivating and maintaining a positive working culture managing over 500 people is not always easy. I began to struggle and couldn't understand why everyone just couldn't get along and do their job. Meanwhile I was working 50-60 hours a week in order to stay on top of everything. I was overwhelmed and growing resentful of everyone and everything around me. One day I recognized that most of these challenges started with MY perception and attitude. Once I realized this and took accountability for my role in my life, personally and professionally, my world started to change.

So how did this great spiritual growth happen? I have been working on my journey for ten years. I have always had my angel cards, positive affirmations and friends that were positive influences, and I bought every book I could that would help me grow. Today I realize that I had all those tools in my tool box, but I never learned or really put them to use. I never truly saw the gifts in my life and my lessons. I did angel cards readings and would look at my positive affirmations trying to keep my spirit feeling positive. I have a whole book shelf of books I've never read! With every "bad" thing that happened in my life, rather than use the tools in my tool box, I chose to be on a pity potty that sometimes was hard to get off. When I did come off the pity potty, I still failed to see the gifts that had been given to me with each lesson. I could never understand why I always felt so tired and drained. I felt everyone around me was taking and taking ... never giving me anything in return. The dreary side of life had taken over. I was overcome with every day duties, busy schedules, and I habitually neglected myself and my spirit.

As is the case with everyone, I have had many trials and tribulations to contend with. How do we work past them? How do we continue moving forward, while still honoring ourselves? Sometimes life has speed bumps along the way. I have learned to go over them slowly and work through it. The speed bumps are there so that we can slow down, learn to enjoy the journey and reflect. Soon you will say: "Wow, I am so glad I had that lesson." You must show gratitude for the lessons in order to grow and move forward. Without the speed bumps in life, you can miss many lessons, and you will continue to have the same lessons until you have learned what you need from them. You must show gratitude for these lessons, and in doing so, you will reap the benefits of growing and moving forward.

It was not until recently that I was forced to reawaken to my journey. January 30, 2012, I tragically lost the love of my life. He has three beautiful boys who have lost one of the most important people in their lives. It was through this tragedy that my greatest growth has happened, and my purpose has been truly defined.

At his funeral Sunny said, "You must find the gifts with this tragedy." I was so angry, thinking: "What do you mean gifts?" Eventually, with every moment, I started to see the gifts of life. I thought about what Sunny had said every day that followed. I always thought I was a grateful and humble person, but I now know what genuine gratitude and humility are. The gifts that stem from feeling these emotions are grand! Once this happened, everything started pouring in abundance all around me.

I realized the love of my life who had passed was and would continue to be my greatest teacher. When he first passed away, I was angry at him for committing suicide, and then my anger quickly turned to the world. Everywhere I went I was hurting. I saw people all around me not having compassion for one another. It was killing me to see the judgments placed on each other and the lack of love shown towards each other. As our family was healing, everyone had varied emotions. Throughout this tragedy, people were showing anger towards one another. This taught me patience and compassion to try and understand their pain and to love unconditionally.

With this new found gratitude and humility, I do not let anything pass by without saying "thanks." I notice every little thing. My spirit is speaking to me, and I am now listening for a change. I know my spirit has spoken before, but I chose not to listen. Yes it is a choice! Now I slow down and take time to visit my spirit. I have learned it is not only okay, but important to take care of myself first. If we do not take care of ourselves and take time to nourish our spirit, we are no good for anyone. In the past, I would feel like if I took care of myself first, it was a selfish act. It is not selfish, and it must happen in order for you to hear and see the world in the way it was meant for you see it.

I still wanted to change the world. I still wanted to make the world more compassionate. Yet, the thought of changing the world in some important way by myself was intimidating. As a result, I started to work on ME. I surrounded myself with spiritual teachers in the form of friends. I made conscious choices to see the signs given to me. I started living my personal journey, started living a more daily positive lifestyle. I started doing things for me, things that brought me great joy. With all of these things, my vibrations started to rise. In the past, my vibration would rise only to crash back down. Now, no person or event brings my vibration down. My vibration is protected as the angels protect me on my journey. If I did not keep filling myself up, then my vibration would fall. Do the things that bring you joy!

Be the change you wish to see in the world

~ MAHATMA GANDHI

This idea was so profound for me. I no longer had this huge responsibility of changing the world. This gave me an intense sense of relief; I could concentrate on only myself. Whew ... what a relief, my journey was just made easier! The changes I have seen around me as my vibration not only rises but stays high have been amazing. Here are the most important pieces I have discovered that have helped me on my journey to renew and understand:

- ➣ I am only responsible for MY own journey. I need to respect that each person has their own journey, and I should not interfere by trying to control, fix or change anything in their journey. Trying to guide someone else's journey does not help them grow and learn the lessons meant for them. In fact, it hinders your own vibration and journey.

- ➣ It is really none of my concern what other people think of me. I was always afraid of judgment from others. Now I think, "It is really none of my business what other people think about me." I live my life in such a way that if someone did say something bad about me, no one would believe it. I do not pass judgments or make negative comments about anyone. If someone comes to me with a negative comment about someone else, I try to help them see the side of compassion and understanding.

- No more negative self-talk! You would not talk to your higher being or your best friend that way. Why talk to yourself that way?

- When someone has feelings that are trying to "hook" into you, anger or judgment for example ... realize that they own those feelings not you. It's their issue not yours!

- Forgiveness is the key to your freedom. Quit dwelling on the past and move out of victim mode; this only adds power to those that have hurt you. Take the power away ... forgive.

- Get rid of all the fear in your life. It only holds you back!

- Keep your vibration high. Others will rise to it.

- Take responsibility for your actions (or inactions). Be accountable and know you have choices. You can choose to stay where you are or you can choose to move up.

- People often ask me, "How do you think positive when there is all this negativity around you?" My response is ... you always have a choice. Yes, you are making the choice. You can make a choice to stay in the negative world around you, and by doing so, you are attracting more of it! You can make a decision to stay in the positive world – baby steps, my friends. Start with a little bit every day, and you will soon no longer see the negative you once saw. Start with daily affirmations, get rid of the negative self-talk that we sometimes don't even realize we do. Turn off the television and turn up the beautiful music, or simply learn to sit in quiet and hear yourself and your spirit.

- Find balance in work and home life. This is the key to keeping your vibration up. Set healthy reasonable boundaries in all areas of your life. If you find balance you will find more joy!

Now that I am continuing to rise on my journey I am starting to see everyone around me raise their vibration too. They are starting to be more kind to each other, to themselves, and to see and live the positive things within their own journeys. Some are learning from me, wait ... does this mean I *AM* changing the world?

This is my purpose. I am an Earth Angel here to help teach the world to love unconditionally in whatever small ways I can. I am mindful of every speed bump I encounter and the lessons to be learned crossing them. Without the speed bumps you will not experience the joy of genuine gratitude and humility which brings much abundance to your life.

 Life isn't about finding yourself. Life is about creating yourself.

~ GEORGE BERNARD SHAW

So I ask you, what are you creating today? Are you creating opportunities to discover and live your purpose?

This chapter is dedicated to Mike Howard, my greatest teacher, and his children: Michael, Sinjin, and Brennan.

Thank you to Sunny for this amazing opportunity, guidance, and support in my life. Thank you to all my angel friends and family who are always there to support me and be teachers in my journey. And, thank you to Symon who has shown me that it is safe to love and be loved again.

~ Kim Richardson

Our prime purpose in this life is to help others. And if you can't help them, at least don't hurt them.

~ DALAI LAMA

Kailah Eglington

KAILAH EGLINGTON is a motivational speaker, coach, mentor and author, who, through sharing her own personal experiences, helps empower individuals to transform their lives and become the people they want to be. Founder of Life Seeds, she teaches how positive thinking, forgiveness, gratitude, and reconnecting to our Divine wisdom can help individuals overcome physical, emotional and spiritual adversity.

She resides in England with her husband and two cats, where she enjoys writing, quilting and helping others find inner peace and serenity through Reiki, Meditation and spiritual counselling.

ke@lifeseeds.co.uk
www.lifeseeds.co.uk

Walking Your Talk

 "The meaning of life is to find your gift. The purpose of life is to give it away."

~ PABLO PICASSO

From the moment the seed of your life is germinated and starts to grow, you have a purpose on this Earth. You have a unique reason to be here, a special gift to give and no one else can do what you are meant to do. And deep within your inner wisdom, you know what it is.

Some of us will become parents, some will become doctors or lawyers and others will become philosophers or teachers. Others will be here to learn difficult life lessons while some will simply "be."

Yet for many, acknowledging this deeper sense of purpose can be elusive; stepping into their life purpose may seem fraught with obstacles. Some may choose not to follow their inner wisdom and instead follow a path that others think they should follow, and others may simply choose not to hear their soul calling.

So, if we intuitively know what our purpose is; if we carry a profound sense of something greater within us, then why can it be so difficult for us to step into the life we are destined to live or to embrace the person we are meant to be? How is it we can unconsciously or actively sabotage that which will bring us our greatest joy or the deepest answers to the question of: "Why am I here?"

The answer is simple. It is fear.

What is It We Fear?

 The oldest and strongest emotion of mankind is fear, and the oldest and strongest kind of fear is fear of the unknown.

~ H. P. LOVECRAFT

Fear is the deepest and most primal of all emotions. It is an instinctive reaction to anything that we perceive to be dangerous or that poses a threat to us. It is meant to be a protective mechanism and in its purest primal form, fear can save our lives. The problem with fear, though, is that it can trick us into perceiving dangers that are not necessarily real but are the result of the beliefs we were taught as part of our childhood, culture, religion, school or other social systems that were meant to "keep us in line."

Fear of the unknown, fear of change, fear of not being good enough, fear of taking the first step, fear that we don't know what our true purpose is, fear of failure and even fear of success can all stop us from fully living our life purpose. Because of our fears, we may choose to keep our inner light inside and live in darkness, rather than stepping out of the mould that we or others have created for us and living our Divine and beautiful purpose.

So let's stop for a moment, take a deep breath and take a short journey together into how we might overcome some of those fears.

Letting Go of the Fear

 Our deepest fear is not that we are inadequate. Our deepest fear is that we are powerful beyond measure. It is our light, not our darkness that most frightens us.

~ MARIANNE WILLIAMSON

It is inevitable that fear will creep in from time to time when it comes to stepping into our destiny, but to truly Walk our Talk, we have to let go of fear and take the first step. In his book, *Love Is Letting Go of Fear*, Gerald Jampolsky says that the world we see is the result of a belief system that is not working and that we "must be willing to change our belief system, let the past slip away, expand our sense of now, and dissolve the fear in our minds."

Belief system fear is largely a result of the words and signals we learn, see and hear throughout our lives and that preys on our fears. We are taught things to frighten us into not overstepping the perceived boundaries of life. This teaching turns into that very critical voice we all have in our heads that is constantly criticising, putting us down and filling us with doubt.

For me, I knew from an early age that my life purpose was to help others but I was consumed with fear that I wasn't good enough, and how dare I even think that I could help others?

Throughout the years, I chose to ignore my inner voice with so many excuses: I wasn't smart enough, good looking enough, pure enough, I was ugly, my teeth weren't perfect, my voice wasn't right. As I grew older, this fear was taken over by feelings of intimidation by others that I wasn't qualified enough, and so I began "postponing" stepping into my life purpose by becoming a professional student. I was awarded qualification after qualification, but each time I convinced myself that I needed yet another one and still I held back, resorting to my original fears as well. I would get so close to stepping into my life purpose and then fall at the starting gate.

My friends kept asking me why I wasn't getting started when I could help so many with my experiences. After much soul searching, I saw that my fears were not so much that I would fail but that I would make a difference, have to be in the limelight and that people would see I was a fraud, even though rationally and factually this was not the case. Fear was just consuming me.

I realised that I had to do something, so I went back to the basics of meditating and journaling which allowed me to reconnect with and listen to my inner voice, not the one that was constantly criticising, but the one that was gentler, kinder and more spiritual, the deepest part of my being that allowed me to fully accept what I was meant to do and be grateful for my gifts.

Tap into Your Inner Wisdom

 Deep within us all there is an amazing inner sanctuary of the soul, a holy place, a Divine center, a speaking voice, to which we may continually return. It is a dynamic center, a creative life that presses to birth within us.

~ THOMAS KELLY

Sometimes we get caught in a trap of not living our purpose because we don't consciously tap into or listen to our inner wisdom, that inner voice which is our intuitive guide and our deepest connection to the source of all things. Yet, our inner wisdom unconsciously guides us even when we don't realise we are using it. Have you ever had a "gut feeling" about something, or had goose bumps on the inside when you have felt a connection with someone or something and you didn't quite know why? That was your inner wisdom connecting you to something beyond the physical plane.

Your inner wisdom is also a direct connection to your Higher or Divine Self. Some might call it their essence, the Soul or their gut instinct. Whatever words you use, getting in touch with your inner wisdom is vital in helping you to live a more fulfilling life, to understand and affirm your life purpose, and to keep you both grounded and connected to a greater source.

The best way to tap into our inner wisdom is to meditate as it allows us to step out of the everyday world into a contemplative place where we can find stillness and deepen our knowledge. Meditation quiets the mind and allows us to listen to our thoughts and move into a deeper spiritual awareness. The silence can give us a profound sense of peace and can allow us to connect with and listen to the more spiritual and deeper part of our being. By connecting to our inner wisdom, we can release fears, gain knowledge of and feel better about ourselves, get in touch with our higher consciousness and start to Walk our Talk.

 Quiet the mind and the soul will speak.

~ MA JAYA SATI BHAGAVATI

We should strive to meditate every day, even for just 10 minutes. It is a small gift that we can give ourselves for a much greater reward – that of inner peace and reflection. Let me share with you a wonderful meditation for affirming your life purpose!

Find a place that is quiet and make yourself comfortable. Close your eyes and take a few deep breaths and feel your body gently letting go. Become aware of the natural rhythm of your breath and how your lungs rise and fall without effort. Let everything go and just relax.

Now imagine you are standing in front of a doorway. You know that beyond the doorway is a very special place and that when you walk through the doorway, you will step into your future. Take a deep breath and step through. In front of you is a white light – it is so bright and beautiful and warm. You feel safe and protected, calm and unafraid. Within the light you see a box. This box is a gift just for you.

Open the box and within it you will see your life purpose and what you are meant to do. It makes your heart sing. You feel overwhelmed with the happiness and joy that your life purpose brings you. You feel your body tingle with the excitement and anticipation of starting your true journey!

You can feel any fear you have about your life purpose leaving and being absorbed into the white light. You know now that you are completely safe and comfortable with your life purpose. Close the box and place it back into the light, but know that it will always be there whenever you need to look into it.

As you walk away from the light, thank your inner wisdom for guiding you to your life purpose. Walk back through the doorway and when you are ready, slowly open your eyes and reawaken to your surroundings. How did that feel? Are you ready to take the first step?

Trust the Process & Yourself

 Without patience, magic would be undiscovered
- in rushing everything, we would never hear its
whisper inside.

~ TAMORA PIERCE

Once we acknowledge and accept our life purpose, we need to take our time and understand that we are not on a time clock and that fulfilling our life purpose is a lifelong process. With each day, with each meditation, with each thought, your knowledge will grow enabling you to fully step into your purpose. Just allow the process to move at the right pace. All that needs to be revealed to you will be revealed in the right time and in the right place.

When I finally came to accept that my life purpose was to help people through my writing, teaching and speaking, I wanted to ditch everything, have my first book written, my website ready, my Twitter tweeting, my Facebook liked by hundreds of thousands of people, all within 24 hours! Well, perhaps not so quickly, but I did put pressure on myself to get everything in place in an unrealistic timeframe. The result was that I came upon obstacle after obstacle and so many things were whirring around my head, I was unable to do anything.

Because I was trying to "follow the pack" and fit my purpose in with others' expectations of my purpose, the pressure was leading me to a complete standstill. I was becoming more stressed, more demanding of myself, and I was not connecting with my inner wisdom. I was trying to juggle a full-time job with effectively a full-time life purpose, concentrating on the future rather than the present moment, and I was on the borderline of complete burn-out.

A very wise coach helped me to realise that our life purpose is not a competition, we don't have to make it to the finish line first or even have everything in pristine, immaculate order before we take the first step. By trying to rush things, it will either stop or slow down the process or worse still, knock us off our path onto someone else's.

In order to know what to do and when to do it, we have to learn to slow down, have faith, trust the process and listen to our own hearts and our own inner wisdom. When I stopped struggling, many things came into place and the most unexpected opportunities also came to me as well as a sense of peace and knowing that all would be well.

Be Good to & Love Yourself

 You yourself, as much as anybody in the entire universe, deserve your love and affection.

~ BUDDHA

To enable us to truly Walk our Talk, it is important that we unconditionally love ourselves as it is in consciously living in love that we will be the most powerful.

Self-love is not arrogant; it is a profound knowing that *you are enough* just the way you are right now. It is about accepting who you are, warts and all, because that is what makes you so unique and beautiful, and it is important to embrace your uniqueness. You are *already* whole and complete, and your true self *already* radiates the purest, most Divine light that is meant to shine from you.

So, make a decision to look after your mind, body and spirit every day. Even the simplest of things will nourish and refresh you: take a long bath, meditate regularly, play like a child, dance, journal your thoughts, give yourself and someone else a hug! Do something kind for yourself and someone else every day. Most importantly, tell yourself every day how much you love and appreciate *you*!

Practicing these things daily will help you feel ready and confident to Walk your Talk and to help others do the same. And won't that be the greatest gift you can give to any of us?

 We can only be said to be alive in those moments
when our hearts are conscious of our treasures.

~ THORNTON WILDER

Know your treasures *are* you and within you. May your journey be a joyful one, and may you always know that you are enough.

Dedicated to those who feel a greater calling in their lives – may these words help you let go of the fear and embrace the joy of fully living your purpose.

My heartfelt gratitude to my husband and soul mate Mike for his unwavering belief and support; to Juliet Vorster for her wisdom and faith in me; to Nancy, Lisa and Sunny Dawn for this wonderful opportunity; and to my children, on Earth and in Heaven, for being the treasures that have made my life rich and purposeful beyond all measure.

~ Kailah Eglington

Efforts and courage
are not enough
without purpose
and direction.

~ JOHN F. KENNEDY

Liana Salas

LIANA SALAS is a Certified Life Coach and has a B.A. in Psychology from Arizona State University. She has additional education in positive psychology, nutrition, fitness, education, and spiritual studies. She is currently writing, speaking, teaching and coaching others to create amazing transformations in their own lives.

Liana lives in Glendale, Arizona, where she enjoys spending time with her family, friends, and her rabbit, Thumper. She also enjoys hiking, dancing, drawing, traveling, and adventure activities that take to the sky!

Liana@LianaSalas.com
www.LianaSalas.com

The Flight of Your Life

Roads? Where we're going, we don't need roads!

~ MOVIE: *BACK TO THE FUTURE*

A road is common metaphor for our life's journey. There is a road to happiness. You can take the road less traveled. If your journey through life is a road, you can only go as far as the roads can take you. There can be stop signs, stop lights, and road blocks along the way. I would rather see my life's journey as a flight, because in the sky, there are no limits! I am going to share part of my journey with you.

In my pre-teen years I began having a series of health problems, which eventually included two operations. As a result, I had to be home schooled for parts of middle school and high school. I dealt with bouts of depression, turned to food for comfort and started gaining weight. In college, my health started to improve; however, I gained more than the typical freshman fifteen – at one point weighing as much as 223 pounds.

In March of my final year of college, I decided to make a change. I had graduated from high school overweight, and I did not want to graduate from the college the same way. I wanted to be happy, feel beautiful and not let my weight hold me back anymore. I started making changes to my diet and exercising every day. By the time I graduated in December

I lost 30 pounds. No matter how challenging it seemed, I kept working towards my goal. By the fall of the following year I had lost over 70 pounds.

I had always thought that when I lost weight I would be happy. I used my weight as the reason why I did not pursue any of my dreams. If I was thinner, I would feel more confident. I would take dance classes and pursue acting, two things I always dreamed of doing. I thought that if I was thin I would be dating and have a relationship. As I was losing weight, I started feeling beautiful for the first time. I loved buying new clothes in smaller sizes, and it was fun getting compliments from friends and family. However, once I reached my goal weight, I didn't experience the happiness I thought I would.

I was getting asked out on dates, but I was not interested in any of the men asking me out. I was uncertain of what direction I wanted to take my career. I was applying for jobs and going on many interviews but was not getting hired. Now instead of thinking, when I lose weight I will be happy, I began thinking: When I get a job and have a relationship, I will be happy. I also began to wonder if I would ever truly find happiness.

One day my Mom asked me to go with her to a free workshop at our local public library. The speaker was Sunny Dawn Johnston. Sunny and I had some similar experiences in our lives, including challenges with health and weight issues. I was inspired by her story and how she changed her life. I began taking as many of her classes as I could, on topics such as connecting with the angels, intuition, manifestation, and personal development.

During this time I also met a life coach and motivational speaker, who introduced me to the field of life coaching and the relatively new field of positive psychology. I began learning as much as I could on the subject. I knew right away that this was a field I had to study more and would lead me in the direction I wanted to take my career.

I realized that it had not been the weight that had been holding me back, but my own fears. I started getting out of my comfort zone, challenging myself and facing my fears to overcome them. I started learning that the answers lay within me, not in anything external. If I was looking for my weight, a job, or a relationship to make me happy, then I would never find more than temporary fulfillment. I started to realize that happiness is not something that you find; it is something that you live with. It is something that you carry inside you.

I've always been a big dreamer. Since I was very young I've had a list of goals I wanted to accomplish in my lifetime – a "bucket list." I started checking items off the list, including going sky diving and taking a vacation with my best friend to the Bahamas. I started pursuing some of the things I imagined doing. I started feeling in control of my life for the first time.

I had gotten a job as an academic advisor at an online college. After several months working there, the job had become extremely stressful, and my co-workers and I were being overworked and underpaid. I had just started applying for other jobs when I was invited to interview with an airline to be a flight attendant. I had applied almost a year prior. I had always dreamed of traveling and thought this would be one way to do it. In my group interview I was asked why I wanted to be a flight attendant. My answer was that I was ready for a challenge and an adventure. I got the job and more of an adventure than I ever could have imagined!

Three months after I started working for the airline, I started dating a co-worker. I loved being a flight attendant, traveling the country, meeting new people, and I was thrilled to be in love for the first time. However, our relationship had many challenges. My boyfriend had a chronic health condition for which he was not seeking medical treatment. Less than a year into our relationship, he began getting very ill and struggled with depression. As he continued to neglect his health, he also neglected his finances, and many other areas of his life. I also started neglecting myself, focusing all my time and energy on him.

He started making many life changes that did not include me. I found out he had been dishonest with me about numerous things throughout our relationship, including the medical treatment he said he was seeking. I irrationally hoped that if I stood by him long enough, he would appreciate my supporting and taking care of him, and he would be honest with me and want to plan a future together. I started feeling inadequate. If I were enough, if he loved me enough, he would want to be healthy. I had gained 20 pounds and started feeling depressed.

In the spring, after nearly two years together, I finally made the decision to end the relationship. Even though I knew leaving was the best thing for me, I was heartbroken. I felt comforted that I still had a wonderful best friend, my job and my family. I started working as many extra trips as I could, and it helped me keep my mind off the breakup. I worked trips that would allow me to visit friends or family on my overnights; I paid off all my credit card debt and lost 10 pounds of the weight I had gained. I started feeling better and getting over the breakup.

However, at the end of October, my friendship with my best friend of eight years ended. I always felt as though she was the sister I never had. I thought that we would be friends the rest of our lives. I was once again heartbroken. Now I began thinking, I lost my boyfriend and my best friend, but I still have my job and my family.

Then in November, two days before Thanksgiving, I was wrongfully fired from my job as a flight attendant. It was completely shocking and unexpected. I considered myself a hard worker and a great employee. There had been an increase in sick calls in recent months, and the company attributed this to sick leave abuse among the employees. During this time I called out sick for the first time in almost a year, and the company misinterpreted the circumstances surrounding my sick call. Our flight attendant workers' union told me that if I had called out sick under the same circumstances six months prior, it would have been completely uneventful, with no discipline at all, least of all being fired.

I don't know if I will ever be able to completely articulate all the emotions that I felt. I was angry, sad and felt betrayed. Having just recently paid off my debt, I had planned to start saving to buy my first house. Many of my future plans, including those for furthering my education, revolved around the travel benefits, flexible schedule, and financial security of my job. Most of all, I loved being a flight attendant; I love flying. The airline had become like a family to me. I was devastated. I had lost a relationship, a best friend, and my job, all in less than a year.

I was blessed that I did still have my family. My parents and my brother were very supportive and made the holidays enjoyable. Our flight attendant union was appealing my termination, but this was a process that would take time. I had done all I could do. I had to trust in our union, I had to trust in my higher power, and I had to trust in myself.

I had enough knowledge to realize that this was a divine time. I had a choice. I could choose to focus on what I had lost, or I could choose to focus on what I still had. I had a supportive family, I had my health, and I had time. Since I had paid off all my debt just a few months earlier, I had the financial security to take some time for myself, and not have to look for another job right away. I chose to see this time as an opportunity to reflect, gain clarity, and take action.

I had learned so much, from Sunny, from positive psychology and from the many other classes I'd taken and books I'd read. I understood the importance of loving myself and taking control of my happiness. However, I had to do more than understand these concepts, I had to know them. To be of the highest service to others, I had to fully embrace everything I knew and live it myself.

I started doing things to bring me joy, like hiking every day and taking dance classes. I signed up for a nutrition class that I had wanted to take for some time. In the future, as a life coach, with education in nutrition, I could work with clients from a holistic approach. I got back into a daily exercise routine and started applying what I was learning in my nutrition class to my own diet. I lost the last of the ten pounds I had gained, and then some. I made a physical transformation, but more importantly, I made emotional and spiritual transformations.

I chose to see the value in all my past experiences and be in gratitude for them. Everything I experienced had a purpose. Getting fired was a valuable lesson in forgiveness. I could remain angry and resentful for the choices the company had made, or I could choose to see that the company made a mistake and had the opportunity to correct it. It was also a lesson to take advantage of every day and every opportunity.

My relationship with my ex-boyfriend was a lesson on loving myself. The truth was not that he didn't love me enough. It was that he didn't love himself enough to make his health a priority. Most of all, I didn't love myself enough to know that I deserved to be treated better. I was choosing to be unhappy because I chose to stay in the relationship for as long as I did. I have to take responsibility for my own life and my choices.

When you can find the value in an experience and learn from it, then it has a purpose. Many times the purpose of an experience is to give you an opportunity. It can be an opportunity to learn, to grow, or prove to yourself how powerful you are and what you can accomplish. It can be an opportunity to start a new career or to find a new partner who is a better match for you. You don't have to wait for the New Year or a challenging time. Every day is a new opportunity. What you do with that opportunity is up to you. .

Toward the end of January, a friend and co-worker with whom I had not spoken in over a year heard I had been fired and called me. When she asked how I was doing, I said 'I'm great!' She was surprised to hear me say that. I was surprised myself! The truth was that I *was* doing great! I didn't have my job, a relationship, or a best friend, but I was still happy! Like some airplane flights, I was just experiencing turbulence, and my plans had been diverted.

At the beginning of February, within days after that call from my friend, I got a call from the flight attendant union. The airline was reinstating me as a flight attendant, effective immediately. I would have a clean record with no discipline. I burst into tears of joy on the phone. What could have been nearly a year-long process was settled in just over two months.

The knowledge I gained during this time is far greater than anything I could have learned in a class or in a book. As a life coach, author, speaker and teacher, one of the best things I can do is lead by example. I took what was one of the most difficult times in my life and made it one of the most powerful and positive times. It is my hope to inspire others to realize if I could make changes in my own life, they can too.

In the years since that time, I feel as though I've been flying, and soaring! I maintain my weight easily, and I am the healthiest I've ever been. I appreciate my body for all that it allows to me do, not just for what it looks like. I continue to work towards making my dreams a reality, and I have checked off many more items on my "bucket list."

I am happy. It isn't what I look like, what I weigh, or relationships I have. It is the way I choose to live my life. Happiness is my way of being. I live every day with joy, optimism, love, gratitude and purpose. I am confident in knowing that life is a journey. There are always more lessons to learn and more ways to grow. There are always more ways to fly!

Take whatever experiences your journey brings you and learn from them. Find the purpose and live with purpose. Follow your dreams and work purposely to achieve them. The sky is not the limit. The only limits are the ones you create for yourself.

Just as sometimes flights can have delays, diversions, or turbulence, so can life. Your flight path can change at any time, but you can always get back on course. You don't need roads, you were meant to fly! This is the flight of your life. Sit back, relax, and enjoy the flight!

Dedicated to YOU, the reader – may this book support you on your journey. Know that your life has purpose, and you are worthy of every happiness. You can achieve everything your heart desires!

Thanks to my wonderful parents for supporting me and my dreams. Thanks to Mando, my brother and my friend. Sunny Dawn Johnston, thank you for everything – for all you've taught me, for your support, and now, this book. Nancy Newman and Lisa Hardwick, thank you for this opportunity. Deb McGowan, thank you for your enthusiasm and encouragement throughout my writing process. To all my family and friends, I'm blessed to have you in my life. Thanks to the many teachers and authors who have inspired me on my journey. To everyone that has ever helped me to fly – thank you!

~ Liana Salas

Marci Cagen

MARCI CAGEN is a gentle, loving and supportive holistic healer and spiritual teacher with a private practice in Mesa, Arizona. Marci draws upon her experience as a nurse, life coach, and energy worker to guide her clients and students through various phases of healing. She has helped many people find their personal mind-body connection and listen to their own inner truth. Marci has a unique ability to transform her own inspirational life story into practical tools and knowledge for others to learn and grow from.

When she's not teaching, Marci enjoys traveling with her family and spending time in her garden.

www.marcicagen.com

❧ Feel the Feelings

> How might it have been different for you, if, early in your life, the first time you as a tiny child felt your anger coming together inside yourself, someone, a parent or grandparent, or older sister or brother, had said, "Bravo! Yes, that's it! You're feeling it!" How might it be different for you?
>
> ~ JUDITH DUERK

Have you ever noticed that the more you try to stifle your feelings, the more eager they are to come out?

I used to believe that my "life purpose" was a destination, a point we arrive at in our lives where we can finally feel complete and whole. My destinations have included the perfect career, a soul mate relationship, being a perfect mother and daughter, losing weight, gaining weight, having clear skin, thicker hair, bigger boobs – the destinations go on and on. If only I could achieve these goals, obtain these things, then this feeling of restlessness and uneasiness would dissipate. *Then* I would be okay. *Then* this ever-gaping hole inside me would finally be filled. It was like a semi-truck had driven right through the center of my being, and I was always trying to fill it with a Smart car. I was forever looking outside myself, comparing how I felt on the inside to what I perceived others having on the outside. If only I could have that, look like her, do what she does, then I would be enough.

The only problem is that every time one of those things came to fruition, it was still not good enough to fill the void within. There was always something else to do, something more to obtain, someone else to become. One situation after another, one more relationship, one more idea, one more quick fix and then I would finally be living my purpose, right? What I have realized since then is that in all the comparing myself to others, I never once considered the inner feelings they might be having.

I have felt many times in my life that I was the only soul on earth who was experiencing feelings of complete and utter chaos. I spent a lot of time and energy making sure that everything looked okay, and as close to perfect on the outside so that no one would know just how crazy, alone and afraid I felt on the inside. I would do anything I could to avoid feeling these feelings and, more than that, make sure *you* didn't know I felt that way either.

Growing up in an alcoholic and co-dependent home, I learned at a very early age that if I could just control how others were feeling around me by getting good grades, cleaning everything perfectly, looking a certain way, becoming an award-winning athlete, there would be no reason for people to be upset anymore, and I would not have to feel the anger, frustration, shame, grief or fear. Maybe then the fighting would stop, and we could all just be "normal."

The problem with that was, of course, that I could not control how others around me were feeling. Plus, I would pick up everyone else's emotions and absorb all of their stuff, which just added to everything I was already feeling. Somewhere in the midst of all of this, I assumed responsibility to fix everyone else so that I could feel valued and appreciated. The only catch was that I was not allowed to feel any negative stuff because then people would judge me and see that I was out of control, and the world around me would fall apart. So any time I felt angry, afraid, upset or alone, I created a safe place in my imagination and became someone else. I would read books, watch television, and eat whatever I could find. I also got relief from these feelings when I would participate in sports and running. I am sure that is because it helped to move the energy.

I have also tried many other forms of escape from my feelings and self-judgment like shopping, eating, not eating, relationships, alcohol, drugs, you get the picture. Unfortunately, all these created was more self-judgment and the big "S" word. No, not that one, but shame; which come to think of it, can create a lot of … fertilizer. And boy, has it helped me grow!

Shame comes in many forms of concrete and steel, evoking a self-made prison. It separates me from others, it keeps me awake at night, it tells me I'm not good enough, it holds me back and tells me not to even try, it tells me I'm the only one that feels this way and mostly it dims my light, causing me to forget who I truly am.

I used to confuse strong, so-called negative emotions as being bad or not very spiritual and in so doing would immediately judge them, push them down and hide them. That created shame and feelings of not being good enough. I thought if I actually felt the jealousy, anger, or fear, that I was not worthy of Spirit's love. I also believed that I was only supposed to share happy, positive feelings with others because if I showed all of my true feelings, you would see who I really was and that I didn't really have it all together, which I was sure would cause me to end up alone. I was constantly trying to be what I thought everyone else wanted me to be. I became a great chameleon.

Shame has even created physical illness in my body in the form of urinary tract infections, chronic sore throats, extremely painful periods, stabbing pain in my back and so on. Several years back, I encountered a wonderful class with Sunny and a book by Louise L. Hay entitled *You Can Heal Your Life,* which shed some light on the reality that our emotions are directly correlated with pain and illness within the body. It opened my eyes to a whole new world and empowered me with tools to take responsibility and create health, abundance and inner love in my own life.

As a nurse, massage therapist and energy worker, I have seen these illness manifestations firsthand and have come to believe that feeling emotions, whatever they are, is the key to a happy and healthy body, mind and spirit. Put simply, these emotions are just energy in motion or e-motion. The body is made up of billions of electrical impulses, chemicals and matter. I like to think of the central nervous system as being a super highway with many different streets and passageways to various junctions in the body. When we are fatigued and not getting enough nutrition, it's like a construction zone taking place and although things are still moving, it is slow. Stress and inactivity just add to the "traffic." When you throw unexpressed emotions into the mix, it is just like a pile up at five o' clock. The energy or e-motion becomes trapped and stagnant. Physically, we can experience this as tension, pain, knots in the muscles, cravings, or acidic stomach, just to name a few.

When you add in the fact that I was constantly giving away my energy to please others or using it to hide my feelings, all of this made the perfect breeding ground for disease and more fear. In my experience, unexpressed emotion can even cause cancer.

The body is our greatest barometer. It will always tell us what it needs. We just need to pay attention. Think back to a time when you entered a room where someone had just been arguing. You didn't even have to hear a thing, and yet you could still feel the tension, right? Perhaps when you first meet someone, you are immediately drawn to him or her, or you may feel like you can't get away fast enough. This is your body's sixth sense. This is the wisdom from within, and these feelings will be heard one way or another.

Looking back, I can now see where expressing my emotions has been the greatest asset to connecting with others. Just when I thought I was the only one, I let down my guard and allowed others to see all of me, the *real* me. And in so doing, not only have I healed, this willingness to be seen has created space for others to feel comfortable in letting themselves be seen and healed. Those dark and uncomfortable feelings I would not allow others to see within me have been the bridge to profound and meaningful relationships. Most importantly, crossing this bridge has also allowed me to fall deeply in love with myself. I no longer need the opinion of others to feel valued and appreciated. I am responsible for acknowledging my own greatness and showing myself appreciation. I do this by participating in activities that make my heart leap with joy. One of my favorite activities is playing with my dog or going to the dog park. You just can't have a bad day at the dog park!

Since we are beings with a mind, body and soul, it only makes sense that we need to feed all aspects of ourselves. Some of the tools I have used to heal myself include journaling, making sure to express *all* of my feelings, eating nutritious foods, spending time in nature, practicing yoga, receiving regular massages and energy work, meditating in the bathtub, listening to music, singing and dancing.

Using positive affirmations on a daily basis has been monumental in changing my attitude toward myself and others. I use a dry-erase marker to write them up on my bathroom mirror and then repeat them as I am brushing my teeth and putting on my make-up. I also post them on sticky notes all over the house and repeat them throughout the day. When I first wake up, I spend some time in prayer and give thanks for the day. Then I ask my angels to guide me to be of maximum service. Finally, I stretch my arms really wide and affirm "I am open and receptive to all that is good!"

When angry, I write, scream (usually in the car with windows rolled up), hit pillows, put my feet in the grass, and spend time in my garden. Of course, it is of the utmost importance that I communicate my feelings with others in appropriate and non-harmful ways. So when I can speak calmly, I use phrases like "I feel_____ when you_____. All of these actions allow any feelings that can build up and cause me to feel stuck, to be felt and then released, making room for new experiences.

I also feel it is extremely important for me to maintain my own energy. I can observe others and what they are going through, and I can certainly sympathize and relate to their feelings, but I don't have to absorb them anymore. That is a choice. My choice. One of the tools I use in maintaining my energy is asking for help from Archangel Michael. He is the angel of guidance and protection. I invoke his presence every day.

I also have a visualization that I do when I feel myself getting "plugged in" to someone else's emotions: I imagine a power outlet in their abdominal region and visualize myself removing my plug from their socket and plugging it back into myself. I then imagine sending them unconditional love in the form of pink light. This does not mean that I don't care or that I cannot support them, it simply means I am taking back my own power, maintaining my own energy. Loving someone unconditionally does not mean I have to like everything they say or do. It certainly doesn't mean I have to approve of their behavior either. It just means I can hold space to love them exactly where they are in that moment without losing any of my own energy. This exercise has taken a lot of practice, but truly works *when* I choose to use it.

Today, when I think of my life purpose, I can see that *all* of my experiences and *all* of the feelings that I have felt throughout the years have guided me to my true purpose: to create the life I want to live and love myself and others unconditionally. So I say, "Yes, that's it! You've got it! You're feeling it! Bravo! Now keep going!"

This is dedicated to anyone who has ever felt separate from others. May my words be a bridge for comfort and grace to enter your heart and reawaken your soul to the Divine truth that we are never truly alone.

Many thanks to all those that made this book possible. To my students and clients, I stand in deep appreciation of your courage and wisdom. To my parents, I am eternally grateful for your love and support. To my husband, Burton, thank you for believing in all of my dreams. For my son, Skylar, thank you for being my greatest teacher. To the God of my understanding, THANK YOU!

For all the women who have walked the path before me, and have held my hand along the way, there are no words ... only feelings.

~ Marci Cagen

As your mind
becomes clear, so
does your path.

~ SARAH MCCRUM

April L. Dodd

APRIL L. DODD, M.A. had her first spiritual experience at age three, which triggered her life mission to inspire others and live by an adaptation of Erma Bombeck's quote: "When I die and go to Heaven, I want to be able to say to God, 'Phew! I used EVERYTHING you gave me!'"

April has a Master's in Spiritual Psychology, is an inspirational speaker, Senior Executive Coach with Ascendte Advisors, life coach and author, and has served as a confidante, guide and partner in the personal development of thousands, including children, professionals and life enthusiasts.

April resides in Austin, TX, with her husband and two children.

april@aprildodd.com
www.aprildodd.com

✿ Compass in My Pocket

My first experience of divine intervention came to me at the age of three in the front yard of our small house on Syril Drive, in Geneva, Illinois. The day smelled of springtime, that April of 1974. It was my birthday, and being a nature lover, I snuck away from the big family celebration to go outside to show my new toy to my Mother Nature friends, Big Tree and Blue Sky. As I held out my toy in grand appreciation, I suddenly felt overwhelmed with happiness and declared aloud, "Life is SO great!" I couldn't help it. It's all that was in me to say. When I turned toward the loud drunken boisterousness that defined my family, I turned back to nature's beauty and asked, "Why doesn't everybody get how *great* life is?"

In that instant, I came to believe I was here to show everyone how great life is, especially my family. It was like God smiled with me in that moment, infused me with purpose, and with Sky and Tree as my constant witnesses, bequeathed to me my divine order. I knew why I was here. I stood in the holy ground of this experience for a moment, the deep sound of this sacred conversation echoing inside my own private universe, then I turned to go inside to join my family, new toy in my hand, new purpose in my heart.

My purpose became a compass. I saw myself as being responsible for keeping it safe in my pocket and checking to make sure it didn't fall out along the way. I took this compass with me wherever I went. It became my anchor when things got hard, and my friend when I got lonely. It informed and colored everything I did, from how I played games, to whom I played with, to what activities I engaged in, to how I studied at school. At that time I didn't carry a complicated reason for my being. I never had to explain myself, and I just enjoyed unfolding into the beautiful young being I knew I was born to be.

The great poet, David Whyte, asks, "Are we prepared to live in the world with its harsh need to change us?" I wasn't. One morning, while walking to school with a second grade girl that I admired, I was doing my usual singing, and saying good morning to passersby, when she stopped me, looked me straight in the eye and said, "You're ugly, have a rotten voice, and a rotten smile." I believed her. I had dropped my compass.

For twenty-some years, I lost my way. Deep down I knew life was great, but most of the time I worked to hide my light. Because of my experience with this second grader, I believed that being myself and showing how great life was would leave me shamed, without friends, and unlovable. I felt too threatened to live out my divine order. So, I chose a double life, hoping, in some way, to stay connected with what I knew to be true about me.

On the inside I knew life was great, but on the outside I did not feel full permission to express it. On the inside I knew I was pretty, but I was too afraid to show it for fear someone wouldn't like me, and I hid my beauty for most of my life. I stopped smiling. All my school pictures show a closed smile, hiding my teeth behind a thin line. The guards at the roller rink caught onto my double life and called me "Smiley" because I sometimes couldn't hide my smile fast enough behind my small hands, eyes still beaming with giggly joy.

And, I stopped singing, at least in front of anyone. Instead of singing, I hid behind a flute, and became so good at it that I was first chair almost every year through getting my music degree in college. It gave me a lot of attention as I sat in that front chair for every concert. I was so close to being seen, yet I only managed to send out S.O.S messages about life's beauty through the emotive melodies and flying solos I floated out into the audiences that I let appreciate my gift, but stayed invisible enough that they would not judge me for it.

I was seduced by this safety, satisfied with my own story, and for many years of teaching music to children, I was happy. The children were a mirror to me of the child I had been, my own Little April, full of life and joy. I became one of the "favorite" teachers in school. I made it my mission to show them how great life was through music. I danced on my desk with clown shoes on and sang with a red nose to an audience of kids who could care less whether or not I sang on pitch. I created musicals for kids to stand up and face their own fears about being on the stage of life. Kids of all grade levels began coming to me to talk about their problems and their dreams, and so did their parents. I created programs for kids to explore deeper questions, and a brown bag lunch class for parents to learn how to communicate with their kids (which really was about how we communicate with ourselves first). And secretly, I began singing ... to a packed house of well-dressed hangers in my closet.

I could still hear the whisper of that deep sound that had been singing to me since my third birthday when my own unique purpose had been handed to me. Now, as it began to unfold to me, I became aware that there could possibly, *possibly*, be a more fulfilling direction ahead. My inner self began to lose interest in the work that I did, and I began to fall apart.

I brought some of my most important concerns to my spiritual teacher. We took a long walk before resting on his porch swing where I downloaded that "I hate my job, I hate my home, I hate my boyfriend, and I hate my hair! I pray with my forehead to the floor! What in the world do I have to do? Is there some *special* question I need to be asking in order to get some sort of answer!?"

He swung quietly with me as my years of frozen dreams melted into a shimmering puddle on my lap. Then he simply patted my knee, got up, and said, "I'll be right back." He came back with a big blue book in his hand, put it in my lap, and proceeded to tell me how this book, *The Course in Miracles*, came into being, and how it, if I committed to doing the daily lessons, whether I believed them or not, would change my life. We walked up the street to the local bookstore and bought what would soon become my personal bible. As I thanked him and began to head home to begin immediately, I asked him why, after all these years he hadn't told me about this book. He smiled with his eyes and said, "You never asked. Oh, and April, don't change everything at once. Start with your hair."

About the same time, I decided to attend a master's program in Spiritual Psychology to take my compass out of my pocket and finally claim this purpose of helping others see how great life is. Despite the University's unusual application process, I made up my mind I was going. They just didn't know it yet. I had booked my hotel reservations and my plane tickets from Texas to California before I was even accepted. I even prepared a speech in the case I'd have to bust into the room to tell them exactly why they wanted me in this program. I didn't have to use it. My letter of acceptance came the morning I flew out for the first night of class.

The beauty of this two-year program is that instead of a thesis at the end, we did a Life Project. We had to choose something we've always wanted to do but hadn't because something had gotten in the way. Me, I had wanted to be on stage, singing in a musical, but instead I had been hiding behind a flute and taught other kids how to get on stage. This time, it was my turn.

I did everything on every level I could to make this dream come true. On the physical level, I took dance lessons, acting classes, and voice lessons. I cracked, I croaked, and I choked, but I loved every minute of it. On the mental level, I created, memorized, and repeated just one powerful affirmation statement that I said one hundred times in a row, every day for thirty-two days in a row, and then used it whenever I caught myself acting against it. At night, I imagined having conversations with the little girl April who still existed inside of me, and I rebuilt our relationship to one of trust and confidence. I healed old memories, learned the art of self-forgiveness and forgiveness of others, and I began to see that how I related to the issues I believed I was having *was* the issue. Spiritually, I opened myself up to God's assistance to creating this dream or something better for the highest good of all concerned. I saw the world anew.

By the end of the second year, I was nervously driving to my first audition. I knew that I couldn't control the outcome, but I was in charge of how I showed up, and THAT I showed up. What mattered now was that I was doing my part with the greatest self I could create at that time. The rest was up to God. The piano accompanist didn't come, and the girl who sang before me, sang the exact song I had prepared. Not knowing audition etiquette, I thought it was "illegal" to sing the same song. I panicked. Too late. My turn. Taking a second to close my eyes, I repeated my affirmation, "I am enthusiastically expressing my exuberance, radiating my divine light, inviting the hearts of others to sing with me. I am enthusiastically...." Breathe. Now go.

I stood in the middle of that floor, the director's table about 30 feet away, and belted out *Nothing,* the song about a girl who was teased for her singing, but ultimately realized *they* were nothing. When I finished my last lilting line, "...and I felt nothiiiiiiiing!", there was silence. *Sheesh,* I didn't know what to do with silence. The director was looking at my inadequate acting resume. Then he looked up at me, then down again to the resume. Looking up once more he said, "Soooo, have you *ever* been in a musical before?" I walked up to the table, and with shaking hands attempted to point out on the resume the part of the teacher I "starred" as in the school play I created. He looked at it politely. "So, you've *never* been in a musical before, have you?" *Shit. I'm a goner.* "No sir. I haven't." Ready for the rejection, I imagined my inner Little April hugging my leg with more positivity than I could muster myself, as I braced for words of dismissal.

The director looked up at me, took off his bifocals, and said, "You mean to tell me you've been hiding that voice for this long?" Enter cymbal crash, timpani drums, and the Hallelujah chorus. I just about fell to my knees and cried. These were the words I had been longing to hear my whole life. This moment was all mine. I screamed all the way down the highway, window open, new hair flying. I got a part in that five-woman show, named *A...My Name is Alice*, and I got to play a sexy woman, a bitter poet, and a little girl.

Whenever it was time to go on stage as the little girl, I'd take a minute to close my eyes and connect with that little first-grade April inside and say, "Ok, Little April, it's your time to shine!" In that moment, my voice would change to become the voice of the little girl inside who was only waiting to come forward to announce a return to that original knowing of that fateful spring day of inspiration and recognition, as if shouting, "Hey, My Name is *April*!" I was living on purpose.

As I took my final bow as the curtain closed on our last show, I took a picture in my mind of this moment so I could remember it forever, telling myself, "I could die now. Everything else from this point forward is just bonus." Soon after, I left my teaching career and began a private practice of inspiring others through life and executive coaching. I married the man of my dreams and gave birth to a beautiful little girl, whom I aptly named Grace.

One of the things that my spiritual teacher admonished was to "Let that go, too. Because life has a way of heaving a dark night upon us that feels as if even God has abandoned us."

This night came upon me six years after the final curtain call of my last show, when I was about to turn 40, and two-and-half weeks after my son was born. When I called the doctor to tell them about my son's cold symptoms, I thought they would just prescribe something for his cough and sniffles, so I did not expect a rush to the ER that cold Sunday in February. He lay there limp atop what looked more like a pedestal than a bed in a dimly lit pediatric intensive care unit with 20 some tubes and machines attached to him, breathing for him, as he fought a severe case of a virus called RSV. He was the sickest baby in the PICU, but doctors expected him to get better by week's end.

"Listen, he's going to go home and grow up to be the brat he was born to be," the doctor had said. But on the eighth day, my husband held my hand as we sat in a dark cove with the same doctor as the room glowed with a sequence of daily X-rays of Hamilton's lungs, showing progressively more cloudiness each day. The highest level of life support wasn't working, and there was only one other treatment available, with no guarantees. It introduced a slew of other risks and involved a special surgery and a team of people who would be flown in from all over the US.

I sat in the light of those X-rays, the shadow of death feeling so near, my "life is great" purpose feeling further away than ever before, close to a sure defeat. I knew I couldn't run fast enough or far enough to get away from this moment, and I couldn't stop myself from hearing the doctor when he told us that if this last resort didn't work within a week, maximum two, then "I'm sorry. There's nothing we can do."

Oh my God, did he just say that? Hamilton could be gone. I thought: How would I survive that kind of grief?

We asked if they could wait until morning before beginning this potential life-taking endeavor. "Of course," he said, then added, "But I can't give any guarantees about what could happen overnight." I crumbled, but held it together long enough to leave my husband in tears at the hospital while I went home to put Grace to bed.

In the twilight, I sat with only the light of my laptop alive with possibility as I reached out with a prayer request email to the friends to whom I felt most connected, not for help, but to let go of having it all, and to ask only for hope.

The next morning, I received a text from Paul who had not slept at all at the hospital. I paused and held my breath. There, attached to the text, was a photo of two X-Rays. The first was the one taken the day before, clouded and infected with disease threatening to take away Hamilton's life, and the other was clearer, much clearer, amazingly clearer, oh-my-God-I-can-see-his-lungs clearer, and there at the top of that X-Ray was today's date and Hamilton Harrison James Dodd's name. My boy had turned the corner! He'd found his way home, without my compass, but with a determination of spirit that was his own.

I rushed to the hospital and stood by Hamilton's bedside, tears slipping between our fingers as I held those sweet little fat hands. As I stared at his tiny body, I knew his purpose was to live. I realized that instead of living *with a purpose*, I had fallen face first onto the purpose of being. I had lifted my head just enough to find myself nose to nose with this reflection of my Self and the arrow on my compass pointing straight ahead. I had found the part of me that stood with firm eyes, ready to unfold into my own authentic story. Deeper than my audition moment, I was now being shown my real reason for being here. Joy. Pure joy. Being alive because I am alive. Alive with possibility. Just like Hamilton.

Every day isn't perfect, but that still doesn't mean that today doesn't have purpose. Each day has room for joy. It's never easy to *be* the being we were born to be, and it always takes courage to be great. But when given the chance to give up, each of us has an opportunity to astonish ourselves instead. Within the miracle of possibilities I saw that there is no resting place, but there is always a place for me. The purpose of life is joy, and my practice is to keep coming back to joy, no matter what is happening.

I find myself relentlessly listening close for every whisper that connects me to the echo that leads me back to my blue-sky moment in my front yard at age three. When I raised a joyful face and smiled at the Universe knowing it was mine. As I live out this life's purpose, I will see the world through delighted eyes, I will sing, and I will continue to dance all the way back home with my compass firmly in my pocket.

Dedicated to Little April, and the Little Ones in all of us who stand with firm eyes and say "This is where I stand!" To Grace and Hamilton, may you find inspiration in these stories when you feel you've lost your compass. To Bob, because I Remember.

In gratitude to My Love. Your fierce determination to never give up is a rock in my life.

Many hugs of gratitude to the angels of USM who've tirelessly cheered me along the gauntlet of love. Thank you to Bob for teaching me how to start simple and make the Universe disappear.

Thank you to Robin Colucci Hoffman, your belief in my voice taught me to reach deeper.

My client friends and Refiners, thank you for holding for my highest when the fire got hot, and for our courageous journey together to abide in the thread.

Tim, Hatama.

~ April L. Dodd

There is no right or wrong path. There is only the path you choose. Whatever you choose, there will be many opportunities for you to grow and expand.

~ KUAN YIN

Cris Hitterman

CRIS HITTERMAN is passionate about helping others discover their greatness and understand their energy by making the healing and discovery process fun, creative, and transformational! She has traveled around the world learning various healing modalities which have assisted her with releasing 242 pounds, and have guided her in the greatest journey of all: Learning to love Oneself!

Cris is passionate about creating events and opportunities to help people remember who they are, which is simply LOVE ... she recently started a non-profit known as I Am Love to help share this awareness and has also created an angel-inspired jewelry line, Whispirations.

iamlove111@hotmail.com
iamlove@crishitterman.com
www.whispirations.com
www.crishitterman.com

❀ Simply Remember, You Are Love

It has been said that "the greatest challenge in life is discovering who you are. The second is being happy with what you find." From the moment we are born and take our first breath, inquiring minds are already curious about who we are, what we will be, and what our purpose is on this earth. From the moment we are able to communicate, we are asked, "What do you want to be when you grow up?" I find this question to be the most freeing question there is – the ability to dream big and truly give others a taste of who you are, along with freedom to express and discover what you truly enjoy.

At the same time, I find this question to be the most paralyzing question of all. It is a question that requires you to look deep within and figure out who you are, and most of all discover what gifts and talents you have to offer this world – which can be pretty scary to actually realize that you have a value and worth to this world. That your presence does make a difference.

I admit I have always been a dreamer, so this question has always kept me entertained and has always inspired me to explore different pieces of who I am. Being one of academia nature, I for sure thought my purpose in life was, of course, from the selected careers which involved college degrees. Loving to learn as I do, I knew I wanted to study as much as possible. Some people love desserts. I have a huge appetite for knowledge.

I believed my soul purpose was either to become a teacher, a psychologist, or a doctor. These were areas that interested me. I loved to share the knowledge I had just learned through my books or through my experiences. I also loved to grow. I was fascinated with observing people, their ways and their interactions. And last but not least, I was fascinated with how the human body works. I for sure believed that my soul purpose in this world was to be Option A, B, or C.

With this awareness, I decided to follow a somewhat traditional path and to go to school to pursue a degree. With my thirst for knowledge, I began to study everything under the stars, from archeology to zoology. I was changing my major every semester – I had become a professional student. At the same time, I did what I thought was the next best thing and bought a coffee shop at the age of 19. During this time, I believed having a degree, owning a business and having money all equated to having a soul purpose. Well, to make a long story short, I pursued this path for quite some time. The universe helped me out with this one, as I believe the universe could not bear to watch the agony I put myself through. I was like a lost little puppy.

The more and more I pursued this path and belief, the more my world would crumble. (I can be a bit stubborn at times). I had come to a crossroad, where I needed to make a decision to end my failing business, along with decide if I should continue with school, as I was going nowhere. After seven years of this belief, I had nothing to show. I no longer had my business, and not even a degree, due to taking such a wide variety of classes. The only thing I did have to show for myself was that during this process, I had tipped the scales at over 500 pounds. I was so lost and had no idea who I was without school or my business. I did not even recognize myself in the mirror anymore. I had become so focused on living up to titles and expectations, that I lost sight of who I truly was.

The pity party paradise was not working for me anymore. Here I was living with my parents, no job, no money and over 500 pounds. I felt useless to this world. But yet I desired so much to contribute to this world. I knew the only way out of this was to go within and discover who I was. What do you mean I had to spend time with myself? I was disgusted with myself. I was a huge fix-up project. Every morning I felt like I was waking up to a mountain right outside of my door. At this time, I believed building the pyramids myself would have been easier than discovering who I was.

It was time to bring out the alchemist within me because a miracle was in order. I figured if an alchemist can turn lead into gold, then I definitely was going to find a way to turn my hardships and fat into gold. It was through facing my hardships head on and connecting with myself, I began to discover my soul purpose, which had been there all along. My soul purpose was to discover who I truly was and allow myself to live in my truth. My whole life, I was constantly looking outside of myself for a purpose, when all along, I was my own soul purpose. I just had to remember who I was. I had spent a lifetime of conforming myself and my beliefs to what I thought made other people like me and be happy, all along forgetting who I was. My mission was to remember who I am. Which is simply love.

I felt like Alice in Wonderland, and I had stepped through the mirror and discovered a whole new world. I began the bravest journey of all, loving and accepting myself. I began to exercise. I began to study nutrition and connect with food on a different level. I began taking classes in Metaphysical Sciences. I began meditating. I began discovering the rainbow of emotions I had, and learned healthy ways to express these emotions. I began to become aware of my energy and take responsibility for my energy. I began to play and have fun. I seriously entered

Wonderland, as I was full of curiosity. I had no idea there was so much to explore. I had become my own playground. My full-time job and purpose had become me.

I was discovering more and more about me each and every day. I was feeling lighter and lighter. Not just from the weight falling off, but I was allowing myself to experience and express who I truly was. I was having fun. After years of being a people pleaser and a martyr, it was such a weird concept to ask myself what I wanted, let alone to feel so great and have so much fun. I felt selfish asking myself what I wanted as it went against everything I had been taught. I had to learn to change this soundtrack real quick, as this soundtrack was just taking me to the grave – and that, I knew, was someplace I did not want to go.

It took a great deal of effort in the beginning as I was clueless how to even focus and take care of myself. I was so used to always focusing on others and seeing what their needs were. I became my own personal genie with the help of the universe and angels. I was constantly checking and seeing what my needs were, then delivering those needs to my body, mind, spirit, and emotions so that I could heal. It was almost like learning a new language. I had no idea what my feelings were, why I was having certain feelings, or where these feelings were even coming from. Whoever knew emotions could be so exhausting?

It was then I learned the gift of being in the present moment. By being in the present, I was open to spontaneity. I was open to acceptance. So not only did I have to learn to go within, I also had to learn to trust. This meant giving up control, and I really was out of my box on this one. But as I began to give up control, my whole life before me began to transform.

Life became magical almost instantly. I was very happy with who I was discovering, and with the 242 pounds I had released. I admit, in the beginning, I thought I was doing this to release the weight to attract love and better health. It was then that I realized that I had manifested all that I had because I had a deep passion to learn, and to help share with others and help others live their amazing life. I wanted people to feel good about themselves, and realize how truly amazing they were. I wanted people to see themselves as I saw them – simply as LOVE and absolutely amazing. I desired so deeply for everyone to feel just as amazing as I felt and to share this energy with the world. I also desired to have a world filled with this energy. But I could not share this energy with others until I had discovered it within me.

My whole life I had been looking outside of myself for this energy of love, searching for it in other people, not realizing that it was within me the whole time. As Rumi says "your task is not to seek love, but to seek and find all the barriers within yourself that you have built against it." Love is within us the whole time. The answers are within us the whole time. But yet we begin to compare ourselves with others, and begin to mold ourselves to others' expectations, and we forget who we are in the process by thinking we are not good enough. We begin to not trust ourselves, and from a very young age, we begin to create a war within ourselves striving for answers and searching outside of ourselves. Creating a life of barriers. Losing sight of our gift and our value each time we compare and strive for perfection.

Through this process, I realized how amazing we are and what potential we have. As we have become Masters at creating opportunities of war and ways to measure our worth, we have been Masters of denying our true selves. We have become addicted to drama, stress, chaos, and limiting, negative thoughts and beliefs. As the war continues internally, the wars outside and the suffering continue to exist and intensify. We are very creative beings and have become comfortable with the pain and this way of life. But what if we change our focus?

So many people would rather experience pain, or be numb, than experience love. Love is so foreign to so many, but yet is simply our own nature, and our truth. Many addictions have been created to create a barrier from love and pain. But what if we used our creative energy, ideas and ways to create and surround ourselves with more opportunities of love, happiness and acceptance making this world a better place? As Mother Teresa once said, "If you have a war protest, I will have to respectfully decline. However, if you have a party for peace, I will be sure to be there." What if we focused on peace and love, in place of war? What amazing things can you think of to help share with this world which inspire this truth? It does not have to be perfected. It already is. Just share your thoughts and creations with the world. Get them out there. Share yourself.

This is what inspires me to continue my path of loving and accepting myself as I am and creating an abundance of opportunities of love and peace, helping end the war within, and create and live the change I want to see in this world. It is this that inspires me to support people in being themselves and accepting themselves, regardless of their shape, size, bank accounts, degrees, religion or race. We are all one. We are all love. We each have a soul purpose. Our soul purpose is simply to share ourselves with the world. We are not a mold. There is not another soul out there like us.

We are already perfect. We just have to remember that. It is our happiness that tells us if we are on track. It is when we compare to others that we begin to lose sight of who we are and how truly perfect we really are. There is not another you out there. The bravest mission, and biggest contribution you can make to this world, is to simply be you, which is simply love. Take a deep breathe, and just know that you, just being where you are right now, at this moment, is your soul purpose. You are already perfect. You just have to remember that. Just know and remember that **you are love**. If you are feeling anything other than love, then you have forgotten who you are.

Dedicated to those who have yet to discover the angel living within your heart and the diamond that you are! It is time to shine, you cannot hide, this world needs you!

I would like to express my deepest gratitude to my parents, my friends, and the many earth angels and mentors who have supported me in more ways than you will ever know. I would also like to express my deepest gratitude to Shauners, who is not only my brother, but also my role model! Thank you for always being there, and for always being you! Last but not least, I would like to express my gratitude for all the readers like you, who are here to help make this world a better place, and in remembering who you are … simply LOVE! We are all mirrors.

~ Cris Hitterman

Nicole Stevenson

NICOLE STEVENSON is a licensed Heal Your Life® Teacher/Workshop Facilitator, Numerologist, Level 3 Reconnective Healing Practitioner, Natural Health Specialist, author, speaker and overall lover of life. She is uniquely qualified to assist others transcend limiting beliefs, discover their numerical destiny and heal on all levels including spiritual, physical, emotional and mental using all natural remedies.

Nicole lives in Calgary, Alberta, Canada where she loves to spend time with her family and friends. She especially enjoys spending time at the family cabin, reading and traveling to Maui whenever she can.

Info@AromaSage.ca
www.AromaSage.ca

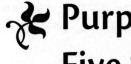 Purposeful Living in Five Simple Steps

L iving your purpose. What does that really mean? Is it different for everyone, or do we all share a common purpose? Am I responsible for seeking out and finding my purpose, or is it something that is found within me? Does my purpose change throughout my life, or are we born with one single purpose that we are meant to work on our entire lives while we are here in the physical? Am I qualified to write about a subject that I'm not entirely sure I'm even doing myself yet?

It was questions like these which consumed my thoughts while I was preparing to write this chapter. I looked for the answers in books, looked at several online websites, asked friends and colleagues and even looked up the definition in the dictionary. I found even the dictionary, as well as other resources, had differing meanings for purpose.

The first definition I found described purpose as being something set up, an object or end to be attained. This definition lends itself to a more materialistic explanation of purpose and for some reason that didn't resonate with me. The second definition, which I seemed to feel more aligned with, described purpose as more of an intention, to propose as an aim to oneself, and felt to me less physical and more mental and emotional.

I had expected the dictionary to solve my dilemma yet it had only provided more confusion, creating more and more unanswered questions about what living your purpose really meant. More importantly what it meant to me. I meditated and prayed that somehow or some way I would find clarity on this subject, not only for the purposes of this book but for myself as well. It took some time but my prayers were being answered, and my own personal definition was about to become very clear.

As the Universe does, it orchestrated the delivery of the perfect inspiration to synchronistically arrive in my experience. It couldn't have come at a better time as I was suffering with what I believe to be the worst writer's block known to humanity. A novice writer and the submission deadline looming only two short weeks away, I was filled with fear, panic and anxiety surrounding what I would eventually write about in this chapter. Needless to say, I was both relieved and sincerely grateful when this golden seed of inspiration appeared to me.

Ironically enough, this message was presented as a Facebook post from Cheryl Lee Harnish, a remarkable author I personally enjoy very much, and it read, "You have not come here to FIND your purpose. You have come here WITH your purpose and FOR a purpose. It is simply the act of allowing your deepest heart's TRUE expression, which is your destiny." Cheryl managed to take all the feeling and emotion behind what I thought to be true regarding my own personal definition of living your purpose and so brilliantly placed them into one, simple yet profound, Facebook post.

I spent the next nine hours feverishly pounding keys on my laptop as I tried to keep up with all the thoughts, words, and expressions of what had just been sparked within me. Now that I know what it means to me to live life on purpose, how do I then communicate it to others? The "whats" and the "whys" are always easier to write about, but I really wanted to share what I believe to be the most significant pieces of the puzzle: the "hows."

How do you recognize if you are, in fact, living your purpose? If you find that you aren't living life according to your higher purpose, then how do you take a hard right and realign with your path? What are the key factors in assisting people to live happier, healthier and more purpose-filled lives? How does an individual genuinely express their heart's true purpose, as Cheryl mentioned. Although I was now faced with finding answers to a whole new set of questions, I felt easily guided to the answers within myself, and the fear had subsided. I trusted that this chapter for me was going to be a journey of new insights and realizations ... perhaps I might create a few new beliefs along the way.

After excavating deep within myself, I have determined that there are very evident steps towards living your purpose in a way that is easy, repeatable and applicable to all who wish to add meaning to their lives. Each step consists of uncovering your own beliefs, and in some cases removing the ones that no longer serve you, in order to establish new ones. I don't claim to have worked out all the kinks, and this is not meant to be construed as an exact science. My intention is to provide you with a framework or a starting point to get you moving in the right direction. If you truly desire to live a life of purpose and authenticity, it's your job to do the work to figure it out in your own unique way.

Step No. 1 – Look Within to Find Your Bliss

 There is no greater gift you can give or receive than to honor your calling. It's why you were born and how you become most alive.

~ OPRAH

It's occurred to me over the last few years that I have a deep desire for more out of my life. I desire to have a meaningful, directed, fulfilling life – even if it means pursuing things that aren't exactly practical, and that may not come easily. As many have experienced before, I have also spent countless nights lying awake trying to figure out what to do with my life. Oftentimes, trying to find the real you and your real desires is the most difficult part of living life on purpose.

This leads me to what I consider to be one of the most integral and important steps towards finding and fulfilling your highest purpose. It's important to ask yourself a few questions when trying to determine what your own personal purpose is in this world. What gets you excited? What makes you feel inspired? In what situations do you find yourself completely absorbed, focused and motivated? When you experience feelings of joy, connection, and peace, these are direct indications that you're doing something that works for you and that feels good. Make a mental note when you find activities that bring you these types of reactions. These emotions represent your inner bliss and will unmistakably guide you in the direction of your heart's true expression.

Additionally, should you experience the opposite feelings like tension, resistance, exhaustion or boredom, these are equally important. They are the keys to helping you realize that which is no longer serving you and is likely taking you away from finding and living your bliss. Don't waste one single moment putting your energy towards these types of activities. Living your purpose may not mean that life is going to be without hard work, determination or sacrifice, and you may have moments where you feel challenged and frustrated. As long as you are in alignment with what it is you are doing and you remain interested and engaged despite the obstacles ... you are on the right track.

Step No. 2 – Activate the Vision

 Destiny is not a matter of chance; it is a matter of choice. It is not a thing to be waited for; it is a thing to be achieved.

~ WILLIAM JENNINGS BRYAN

Now that you've identified what makes your soul soar, the next step to living the life you want is leaving behind the life you don't want. Taking the first few steps forward can be the hardest, but each step forward gets easier and less arduous. Momentum generated from taking purposeful action, even when you are unsure of the outcome, may very well be the most noteworthy step to creating a life of your dreams.

With your recent discoveries in mind, make a list of accomplishments or goals you plan to achieve. These goals can range from person to person and may include having a baby, switching careers, going back to school, moving your home, losing excess weight and getting healthier or even leaving a dysfunctional relationship. Writing, or more specifically becoming a published author, happened to be one of my bucket list items which I'm now able to check off my list. So I can speak from experience when I say the pay off from moving confidently towards your dreams far outweighs the fear of the unknown, judgment of your peers or leading a life of dissatisfaction and regret.

Once you've identified these personal goals, make charts, time lines, or vision boards to keep you on track and inspired. Choose techniques that will keep you focused, motivated and your energy high. We've all experienced getting excited about something new, only to find just as quickly as it arrived it's disappeared, and we are left feeling deflated. I personally find that visualizations and daily affirmations help me address issues of fear and deservability and helps create a clear and positive image of what I'm working toward. These methods get me excited, raising my energy, by imagining my life as if I'd already accomplished my wildest dreams.

Law of attraction specialists encourage us to bring our energy vibration into alignment with the energy vibration of that which we wish to manifest in our lives, and I find that consistently visualizing in this way helps me to reach that objective. When you remove lower energy vibrations from your life, eliminating negative thought patterns, you give yourself the freedom to live in the now and take advantage of all the infinite possibilities you can create for yourself.

Step No. 3 – Feel the Fear and Do It Anyway

 Don't be afraid of your fears. They're not there to scare you. They're there to let you know that something is worth it.

~ C. JOYBELL C.

Fear can be the most limiting and uncomfortable step for many who wish to make changes in their lives. It's natural to want to hide from our fears and remain in our comfort zones. In our attempts to move past fear, we tend to ignore it or suppress it rather than embrace it. Every fear has a specific purpose, and the only way to uncover a fear's purpose is to start by accepting it - by feeling the fear and doing it anyway.

Ask yourself: What's truly going on? What specifically are you fearful about? Take the time to explore your emotions to see what surfaces and gently replace the fearful thoughts with more positive and supportive beliefs. In some cases, fears stem from not being well prepared and can be a tool to signal us to do our homework to ensure we have all the necessary information to move forward. Perhaps it's an issue of building our confidence. Mastin Kipp, creator of The Daily Love, believes "that excuses are just low self-worth trying to take over your life." Believe in yourself!

Fear doesn't have to be immobilizing and can serve as a powerful tool for growth if we lovingly listen to the signals, recognize the emotions behind it and act upon them. Make a conscious choice today to change your mind about fear. When you are feeling your body shake and your heart pound, embrace it, and instead of allowing those feelings to hinder you, use it as your adrenaline rush to boost your passion and drive. You may find that with time and practice you'll learn to love the sensations of fear because it'll propel you to do the things you once thought to be impossible. Remember, this is the part of the process where we begin to grow as individuals and discover who we were meant to be by challenging ourselves to step out of our proverbial boxes.

Step No. 4 – You Are the Company You Keep

 If you're the smartest person in your group, then you need a new group.

~ LES BROWN

Take a good, hard look at your inner circle of friends, family and colleagues. Are you the most productive, inspired, intelligent or successful of those you choose to spend your time with on a regular basis? If so, chances are you need to align yourself with people who are able to give you a fresh perspective and inspire you to think beyond the realms of your normal thought patterns. Choose to associate yourself with people who support and uplift you. When looking for insights or advice, seek individuals who may have embarked on a similar journey. Find a way to place yourself in their inner circle and study their techniques. I'm certainly not suggesting that you become a stalker; however, there are several successful people in the world who are looking to share their gifts and talents ... find them.

On the other side of the coin, as you move steadily towards the life you have now clearly defined, prepare yourself for those who will try to bring you down. It's not that these individuals don't want you to succeed, but your growth and your ability to create success forces them to acknowledge what they aren't doing for themselves. Don't let them dull your clarity or second guess your mission. While some of their arguments may have merit in their lives, they aren't you.

It takes true self-confidence to set out on your own path of living your divine path. No two of us are the same, and no two of us will have the same path and impact on this wonderful world. Recognize this and let it serve as your inspiration and your own personal definition of your life purpose.

Step No. 5 – Repeat

 There is no chance, no destiny, no fate that can circumvent or hinder or control the firm resolve of a determined soul.

~ ELLA WHEELER WILCOX

I've arrived at the conclusion that we aren't born into this life with one goal or target. As we evolve and grow, we aspire to new heights and climb new mountains. Our life purpose must then evolve with us, ever changing and morphing along every step of the way. Repeat these steps as you find yourself faced with new quests and dive a little deeper with each venture you embark upon. Living on purpose is a lifestyle, a way of being and a lifelong spiritual practice that will refine your soul. This isn't a quick fix plan but a lifelong adventure!

What has been so amazing to me in writing this chapter is that I didn't realize the depth of which the Universe will endeavor to help steer you onto the right path. I myself struggled with how to express inner passions and live a life on purpose. Little did I know that being invited to write a chapter in this amazing book would actually help me to gain insight about my own life and the steps that I need to take for my health, my sanity, my happiness and for my life's purpose.

What I've discovered in all the research, preparation and contemplation that came as part of writing this chapter was, while I thought I was merely writing as part of a collaboration for a book, I was in fact remembering all of the puzzle pieces that are me and putting them all back together. I was recalling the life purpose that I was born with and that resides within me despite the conditioning I've been subjected to. I was rediscovering my heart's true desires. I've come to the awareness that there is no definition of purpose - at least no definition that fits for us all. How you choose to show up in this lifetime is your life's purpose and yours alone.

I now have designed my definition of living my life's purpose, created my own action plan and am building a strong foundation for my future success. In this process, I've identified all the areas in which I've been holding myself back and armed with this knowledge, I can embark on a new purposeful journey. I hope you will join me on this journey in which we will honor the individuals we were born to be, embracing our divinity as we begin to live our lives on purpose.

Dedicated to all those seeking their infinite selves through passion and purpose – may you find your own personal definition of purpose that fills you with a renewed sense of how your soul's true expression will present itself in this amazing journey called Life.

Thank you to all those brave enough to step outside the box and open the door to honoring individuality and authenticity. You have inspired me to embark on this adventure of self-realization and allowed me to live my life on and with purpose. I'm especially grateful to my husband and daughter, who at times may have thought I was crazy, and loved and supported me anyway!

~ Nicole Stevenson

The meaning of life
is to find your gift.
The purpose of life
is to give it away.

~ PABLO PICASSO

Dawn Amberley

DAWN AMBERLEY was born and bred an English rose, with an endless passion for helping others overcome their limitations and obstacles. A corporate manager by day, by night her alter ego surfaces by providing compassionate care to seriously ill patients and supporting their caregivers.

Dawn now resides in Phoenix, Arizona where she finds wonder in the sun setting on the desert mountains and inspiration in the starry skies at night. She firmly believes that what you give out to the world you get back – ten-fold, so best make it amazing!

dawnamberley@yahoo.com

❧ What My Body Knew

January 27, 2010

This wasn't what I was expecting to see. It seemed innocent enough, Martyn lying there with a drip in his arm, but this was one of those occasions where my body knew something way before my brain could comprehend. Alarm bells were going off in my head like crazy.

I'd rushed from work to the hospital to collect him and fully expected to find him dressed and ready to go, complaining that he'd had to wait for me. Instead, he was still lying in the recovery bed with this drip in his arm. You have to understand that here was a larger-than-life man that didn't have things wrong with him. This didn't make sense.

I tried to gain my composure and keep my voice up-beat. "Hi babes, what's going on?" "I've got to have an operation," he said. "They found a lump when they did the endoscopy. The doctor has been waiting to talk to you." "Oh, okay ..." I replied in the best even-toned voice I could manage. Now my mind was really racing. The doctor wants to talk to ME? His girlfriend? Although we'd been together for over a decade, we weren't married and in my wildly overactive brain I even had time to consider that maybe the doctor wouldn't think I could be privy to his personal information. How bad could this be that he would wait for me to arrive? *BAD!*

My body took over the controls again and my heart started thumping against my chest. I picked up the report and the photos of the scan and turned away from him to look at the pages. I needed an excuse to turn away so I could hide the tears welling up in my eyes. The doctor then breezed around the corner. "Hello!" He was all cheerful and happy. I put on a big smile and shook my head a bit to try and clear my mind. He picked up the page with the scan photos. "Righty ... so here in the first picture we go into the stomach and the first part of the duodenum, and everything looks good."

I had to giggle a little bit inside. I'd never heard anyone say du-ODD-enum before. I glanced over at Martyn, and our eyes met in instant agreement. It was a momentary reprieve. Both being from England, we had many eye connections over the differences between the two supposedly same languages.

The doctor continued, oblivious to our private joke. "The next picture is the second part of the duodenum where we found an infiltrative mass. We took a biopsy, and we need to do some more tests ... " *MASS!*

Mass sounded so much more ominous than the 'lump' that Martyn had mentioned earlier. My heart had moved from pounding my chest and appeared to have fallen into the pit of my stomach and was bouncing around in there. I felt nauseous. The air also seemed to disappear from the room as I struggled to breathe deeply enough to provide sufficient oxygen for my brain to comprehend the situation. I tried to take some slow deep breaths without alerting Martyn to my impending sense of panic and doom. I needed to absorb the stream of information that the doctor was telling me. I had to get a grip on my emotions.

I listened intently to every detail the doctor mentioned and scribbled notes as fast as I could on the report. He saw three possible scenarios, all of which would result in surgery:

1. Stone in the duct (from gall bladder)

2. Ampullary Mass

3. Duodenal Mass

Martyn was to have a CT scan the next day, his blood would be sent to pathology, including a test for CA19-9 marker levels, and we were to follow-up with the G.I. doctor at his clinic in five days for the results and scheduling of surgery. *WE!*

Here we go again. He wanted ME to attend the appointment with Martyn for the results. More alarm bells. This was all so much information to take in and rather a shock. Considering his symptoms, we thought it would be an ulcer or gall bladder issues. Nevertheless, Martyn was in good spirits and was just keen to find out exactly what was going on and get it fixed.

It all started off so simply. Martyn and I had gone back to England over the Christmas holidays to see our families. He seemed to be burping a little more than usual, but was eating quite normally. We came back in the New Year and within a few days he was getting indigestion-type symptoms along with the burping after meals. Over the next week or two his symptoms got worse. He tried antacids and then some over-the-counter Omeprazole, but they made little difference. He was in a lot of pain after most meals.

"It just seems like the food won't go down," he grimaced. I urged him to see his doctor, and he agreed. His G.P. was very understanding and sent him immediately for an ultrasound and referred him to a G.I. doctor where he got the appointment for the endoscopy within a few days. Here we were part way through January – a new year in which so much had happened already.

That night, once alone, I searched the internet like a woman obsessed! Not satisfied with one result about each of the scenarios, I searched multiple times on every word, exhausting myself reading all the medical jargon and potential implications. My head was spinning. There were so many different possibilities, it was impossible to have any real understanding of the situation until the results came through. It didn't stop me in my quest however, and this would be the first of my regular nightly trawls through cyber space to find answers.

Over the weekend we chatted about his symptoms and what this 'lump' might be. "I think you have an alien in there! We should give it a name!" I smiled, trying to keep the conversation lighthearted. "Let's call it George!" Martyn chuckled. George became another of our private jokes and the subject of most of our conversations.

We talked about the trip to the doctor the next day. We put our heads together, and I jotted down his increasing symptoms so we didn't forget anything important: Low stomach pain. Burping. Pain around ribs, when laying down overnight. Back pain. Even drinking water is painful. Dark yellow pee. Clay poop – just started.

February 1, 2010

Armed with my trusty notebook and 'George' folder, we headed for the G.I. doctor's clinic. When Martyn's name was called, instead of going to one of the patient rooms, we were escorted to the doctor's office. "I hate having to bring people to this room," the lady glumly stated before she left us to our own devices. "What the hell was that all about!" We both had the exact same words as we turned to face each other. Our fear levels had just leapt up another notch.

It seemed like an age before the doctor came in and settled down with some pleasantries. He shuffled the papers in front of him and announced that there was a 6cm mass on the head of the pancreas which was 'highly suspicious' for cancer. He didn't just blurt it out. It came wrapped with all kinds of information about the issues with his digestive system, but as anyone who has heard the "C word" come out of a doctor's mouth will understand, life stands still at that point. *CANCER! PANCREATIC CANCER!*

How sick can you feel without actually throwing up? Goodness knows how Martyn felt, but I felt as though I had been kicked in the stomach and whacked across the head. With all the research I'd done, I knew there was a chance it was pancreatic cancer, but it just didn't seem possible that could really happen, until those words were spoken. Nothing – not even the incessant alarms bells – could prepare me for this moment. I was in a state of horror and disbelief.

I tried to focus on writing down some more notes: The high CA19-9 marker level. The fact the bile was being blocked hence causing some of his symptoms. Recommendation of a surgeon to perform a Whipple procedure: major surgery to remove the cancer. This was ridiculously hard work just to try and concentrate, but it saved me from becoming a blubbering heap on the floor.

The doctor had contacted the hospital about having an endoscopic ultrasound (EUS) for further diagnosis and to get a biopsy of the pancreas itself. He told Martyn to get his mobile phone out as they were going to call back on that number with an appointment date. Martyn laid his phone on the desk and within one minute it rang! We actually started laughing. This whole scene was quite surreal. The appointment was for the next day. The doctor left us with the thought of praying for a miracle that this was just a benign tumor and not cancer at all, although his face couldn't hide the truth. Neither of us were religious, but we were going to pray hard.

We spent the evening going over and over the scenario at the doctor's office, trying to make some sense out of this non-sense situation. Aside from the obvious digestive issues, Martyn said he felt really well, and he certainly looked just fine. It was unbelievable. This is what happens to other people, surely. Hadn't we heard that said a thousand times? Now it was our turn.

Later on alone, I searched the internet with a new gusto. I feverishly searched every site that mentioned pancreatic cancer. I found the Pancreatic Cancer Action Network and signed up for their mailing list plus requested a folder of information to be sent to me. I learned some grueling statistics: 94% of patients will die within five years of diagnosis – only 6% survive more than five years and 74% of pancreatic cancer patients die within the first year of diagnosis. These statistics have changed little in the last 40 years.

I stared aghast at the screen. A few days ago I had known nothing about the pancreas, where it was or what it did. I had now reached the pinnacle of information overload. The events of the day were bearing down, and I felt like I might instantaneously combust, right there in front of my computer screen. A little pile of ashes left on the chair where I sat. There was only one thing left to do. I had to give up trying to control my emotions, and I let the tears run down my face. I sobbed. Helplessly.

At the hospital the next day, I rushed to see Martyn as soon as I was told he was in recovery and we anxiously waited for the doctor to provide his conclusions.

"Good and bad news," the doctor declared as he came up to the bed. "The biopsy shows abnormal cells highly likely cancerous, but there is no spread to surrounding lymph nodes or adjacent organs. You are a good candidate for surgery." *GOOD CANDIDATE FOR SURGERY!*

In the most terrible of situations, this was the best news we could hear. It was almost music to our ears. We knew that surgery was Martyn's main hope of survival, and here he had been given this olive branch to hang on to. I could see one hundred tons of invisible weight lifted from his shoulders ... and a trace of tears welling in his eyes. I negotiated the drip and monitor wires and gave him the biggest bear hug I could, with every fiber of my being surrounding him in love.

Something changed in that moment. Maybe the stark realization of how precious life is and how it hangs in the balance every second of every day. Maybe the culmination of the stress and worry over the preceding days. Or maybe just that my body knew more all along than I ever dared to let it reveal. I had never really known my purpose in life, but here it was flashing neon signs in my face. I had never felt this knowing in the pit of my stomach so strongly: I knew I was meant to be here. Right now, with this man. In this situation. Caring for this fellow human being. Walking with him side by side on this journey, wherever it would take us.

I just had no idea how tough this journey was going to be.

Dedicated to all the courageous souls who have faced a cancer diagnosis. My heart goes out to you and those close to you. If I could hug you all, I would.

With endless gratitude to my amazing parents: Your unwavering love and support has carried me through my darkest hours.

To my friends and family, near and far: Thank you for being you and letting me be me. I love you all.

To Nancy Newman and Lisa Hardwick: Thank you for making a dream become a reality.

To Martyn: I will always be your angel.

~ Dawn Amberley

Purpose is what gives life a meaning.

~ CHARLES H. PERKHURST

Jodie Harvala

JODIE HARVALA is an Intuitive Consultant, Teacher, Speaker and Dowser who has a talent for creating dramatic events with powerful results!

Jodie believes that "When energy moves, freedom happens" and by moving energy, she helps others discover they can have the freedom to live the life they intend by connecting spirit, mind and body. As a child Jodie recalls having a heightened sensitivity to the energy of her surroundings and other people.

Today she is Chief Wonderworker of Jodie Harvala and Crew, with an office in Fargo, ND.

Jodie@JodieHarvala.com
www.JodieHarvala.com

When Energy Moves Freedom Happens

When we are living our purpose, the natural occurrence in life comes through to help us move through the blocks that stop us. The right people show up, the right book, the stranger on the street, the exact right experience will show up to show us our way. As a psychic, teacher and dowser, purpose to me is freedom in my daily life.

I grew up feeling trapped inside. I always knew there was a purpose for me, and I knew it would be big, but I had no idea where to find it or how to get to it. I felt like I was supposed to remember something but would run into walls instead. I can look back and see those walls were actually doors that opened and led me exactly where I needed to be. I never thought I would be doing psychic work when I grew up. NEVER. The work I do with spirit is that thing that I needed to remember.

After high school I started working in a nursing home. I worked with the Alzheimer's floor, and it was one of those experiences that I thought to myself - why am I doing this? I would get to work and have to run to the bathroom to cry because I felt so much sadness, but had no idea why. This was one of my first introductions to how I picked up on others people's feelings.

We had two residents who particularly struck me ... a beautiful woman and tough old guy. They each were living on our floor, and for whatever reason they thought they were married. They would hold hands, whisper to each other, flirt, and give each other kisses. The man, however was still married, and his wife would visit often. She would stand to the side and watch the affection they would show each other as he would forget who she even was. It was heartbreaking, and I could feel it. Each day she saw them I could feel it in my heart. I always wondered why I was working in a nursing home at such a young age. What was I learning? A few years later I found out.

My grandpa was diagnosed with Alzheimer's a week after President Reagan. My family was crushed, of course. We watched the decline, and I would offer what I knew of my experiences. That was another clue to my path. I learn by experience, and later figured out I taught by experience. Helping the family through the transition of moving my grandpa out of the house and into a nursing home was both horrible and a relief. I was so thankful I knew what was going on. Little did I know that shortly after my grandpa passed away ten years later (a week before President Reagan), that my grandpa would deliver a message I would never forget.

I sat in my living room with a couple friends who had been practicing their own psychic abilities. One of my friends said, "Hey! Who is that guy that keeps walking from the kitchen to the living room to check on the baby?" I asked if he had a dishtowel over his shoulder, and of course he did. That was my grandpa coming through. Part of the message he gave that night was that he thought it was funny I thought these girls were so talented while working with spirit, and he wanted me to know I would be doing that same thing one day. Four years earlier in my first psychic reading I had heard the same thing!

Little did I know that evening would lead to more classes and more friends in the psychic world, and I would hear those words over and over the next few years as I practiced my own skills. I also ended up on a solo trip to Sedona, Arizona, last year and was able to visit my grandpa's sister. My great aunt was the only other person in my family I had known who had done any type of spiritual work. She let me know that not only did she work with spirit, but it went back at least four generations! What a confidence boost to a new psychic that it ran in the family! I know my grandpa is a guide for me, and because of that one job I had over 20 years ago, it led me to these strings of experiences to help me grow into who I am now. That is what I call purpose!

It seems to me when I think about my life, each job I ever had has helped me in some way on this path. When I sat down to think about this book and what message I wanted to give you, it was that no matter where you work or what you're doing, it all will help with a step later in life. Just when we think we are stuck, the right experience comes along to get the energy moving again. We just need to trust.

My job in radio was also a huge step in my life. I worked as an advertising sales rep. Boy did I have fun! The back end of this story is how I was led to this job. I was in my early 20's and not doing anything very productive after my nursing home job. I partied hard and worked and partied some more. One night sitting at a local bar, I realized it was time to move forward. I needed a job that gave me some pride, and needed it fast.

I ended up calling "Uncle Mike," my best friend's uncle who had had a huge impact in my life since I was young. Even though it was 11:00 at night, he laughed and said to call him Monday as he had an idea for me. I ended up working for him for a little company that sold bathroom ads. You know the ones that you read on the stall door when you're going to the bathroom. I used to call myself the Bathroom Girl. My tagline was "when you pee think of me!" Seriously. It took 10 years for people to forget that line.

I learned how to sell in that job. I learned how to negotiate and how to deal with people. I had grown up super shy, and in that job I needed to either get over it or lose a sale. I learned about self-worth and frustration and success. I was taught about people saying no and me not taking no for an answer.

The two most important lessons I learned was, first, it didn't matter what others thought of me as long as I was okay with what I was doing. Selling bathroom ads was not the scene most people thought of as a successful job. They would laugh and tease and wonder why I was doing a job like that. I LOVED it. I truly loved that job.

Second lesson was if I was having fun I would make money. In this day and age, that's a rare thing for some people. But if I am having fun and truly love what I am doing, I will make money. If I am having fun and am proud of what I am doing, it really doesn't matter what others think of me. This lesson was the most powerful when I started getting into calling myself a psychic. I also learned that doing something that not everyone was doing was way more fun to me then doing what everyone else was.

I owe a great deal to Mike and Steve as they took someone who would walk out at every "no" she heard, to teaching me to stick around and find out why they were saying no.

When I worked at the bathroom ad company, I lived in a teeny tiny little room up in a big old house. Downtown Fargo was a great place, but the homes were old and beat up. I found this place and knew it was perfect as I was starting over. I needed a place of character and cheap! It had a Murphy bed, the type of bed that pulled out from the wall; I thought it was the coolest thing ever!

Each night I would fold it down and jump in! Each night I would pray I would sleep through the night and not get scared. Each night I would put the chain lock on my door, and each night the door would somehow open, and I would wake, but not fully be awake. I would feel scared to death and freeze. I would not be able to talk or to scream and would feel something above me. It was heavy and dense and scary beyond words. I would pray and try to keep breathing, and after a short time I would be able to move my hand or something small and wake myself up and turn on the lights. I would close the door again and wonder what the hell that was! I never really told anyone about it. I also never asked anyone to help figure out what that experience was all about!

Little did I know at that time that later in life I would learn the skill of dowsing, and be able to help others who have that type of energy in the home feel safe and sound. I had no idea how important it was that I was having these scary experiences, and they would later lead to a huge part of my profession. I had no idea that I was feeling a ghost, or energy, or spirit. I had no idea that time in my life was giving me a taste of what was coming down the road for me.

As I write this, I can still feel the fear I had in those moments, and I am so grateful that I now have tools to help others who feel that way. You see, I had to *have* the experience to be able to help others. Sometimes the experiences you're having in life are a way for you to connect to the energy later on to be able to help someone else through the same thing.

Our purpose is to learn and teach. I had no idea how important those times and experiences were, but I can look back now and see the HUGE purpose that each experience had in mind for me. Now twenty years later, I can finally look back and be grateful for all I was taught.

Off to radio sales where I learned all the same lessons from my bathroom ads job but on a larger scale. Again I was working with Uncle Mike. I walked into radio with a big ole attitude, and it worked very well for a long time. I was cocky and had fun and made tons of money. That is, until we moved in with our sister stations, and I was in the midst of the some of the best sales people I know. They were veteran sales people who had worked in radio sales for years and scared the crap out of me. I was totally intimidated by them, and it showed. My sales slipped, and I learned some big lessons around rejection.

I did become friends with my co-workers, and they actually helped me all the time. But I never could find my own confidence inside. My head was too busy listing all the things wrong with me. It took me a while to really step through that and find my way.

Bring in another psychic reading. In town we had this psychic lady who was in a beat-up old home on one of the main avenues in town. I was out selling with one of my co-workers, and we decided to go in for a reading. Way out of her comfort zone, but I was totally into it! This psychic also told me that I would be doing this work!

I remember her place being so run down and knew she was stretching for money with each reading and, for a reason I would find out later, I remembered her set up. I remember her having to leave town because she didn't make enough money to pay her rent. She was very talented but just had not figured out how to make it work financially. She also told me I was in my head a lot and needed to work on my thoughts. If I wanted to make something shift I needed to change my thoughts.

My job had created all this doubt inside, and she wanted me to work on that. How often when we are working on finding our purpose do we forget to listen to the people around us and what they are saying. We may hear them, but we don't always take action. This was the third time I had heard someone say I would be doing psychic work. Again ignored. Lost in the shuffle of life.

After leaving radio, it took me almost a year to recover myself. I used to say I was recovering from working in radio as it is a tough world, but now I can see it was just a time to find myself. Time to find what worked and what didn't work. I think spirit gives us those times in life to have a re-start.

The book, *A Course in Miracles,* showed up shortly after I changed to yet another career in a recruiting agency. I had prayed and asked for a new set of friends. I asked for a community in which I could be supported. An old friend told me about this book, and I signed up for the group and went in without a thought to what it was about. I remember looking at the book and thinking "hmmmm, seems a little out of my league. What have I gotten myself into?" My husband said the same. But he also said "you better go and see what it's about." I agreed and said I already knew I need to go.

I was introduced to the most magical group of people. We were without a doubt brought together to spend an entire year together learning on how to work with the thoughts and beliefs we had. Magical just really doesn't describe that time but it's the only word I can think of to even get close. That year was the beginning of finding out who I really was. I felt unstuck.

When I get stuck I ask myself ok … what is it I am learning? It's just stuck energy, and I need to *feel* why it's stuck. Learning to feel was a huge purpose in all of these experiences. If I didn't know how to feel, I would not be very good at my profession. I teach people how to tap into the emotions of intuition so they in turn can learn to feel their way through life, becoming unstuck and more of who they are.

We teach what we need to learn. I needed to learn to feel, have emotions and how to manage those emotions. My purpose is to have freedom in my emotions. The main theme in my story is about having uncomfortable experiences but learning to work through them and manage my reactions. Stuck energy can always be shifted. I truly believe that. We get to choose the experience to free it. We can do it the easy way or the hard way.

Typically I went with the hard way, the way full of drama and heartache. But these years, most of the time, I can navigate the easy and magical way. I've learned to work with the energy and move through it instead of being stuck in it. When energy moves, freedom happens. When freedom happens, we are in the flow. That is what our purpose in life is about: Finding the freedom.

Dedicated to all those brave souls ready to show up and create the freedom within yourself.

Many thanks to my Husband, Eli, and my children, Foster and Keaton, for showing up in my life. Thank you to all the teachers who have helped me see life in a different way. Thank you to Sunny Dawn Johnston for reminding me to feel my way through life instead of thinking my way through. This has been a great adventure that will lead to so many more!

~ Jodie Harvala

Shellie Couch

SHELLIE COUCH is an author and creator and owner of Practice Living Joy, where she provides group and individual coaching and workshops on the art of living with joy in the present moment. She is often called upon as a speaker on the topics of the power of joy and overcoming personal obstacles.

She resides in rural Inman, Kansas with her husband. She enjoys spending time with her three adult children and her two grandchildren. When not writing or teaching, she enjoys spending time traveling or reconnecting with nature.

shellie.couch@practicelivingjoy.com
www.PracticeLivingJoy.com

ꙮ Red Shoes

What girl doesn't love shoes? I remember, as a young girl, absolutely loving the late part of the summer because that meant back-to-school shopping, and that meant new shoes! Oh, I loved all of the back-to-school shopping experiences and goodies. New binders, fresh clean spiral notebooks, brand new boxes of crayons, unsharpened pencils, new clothes – but the shoes, oh how I loved the shoes!

I can vividly remember one year being so excited because I got red shoes. I am a Kansas girl through and through and always have been. I wanted those shoes, those cute little red patent leather shoes that were shiny, because they reminded me of Dorothy's shoes from *The Wizard of Oz*. They weren't glittery and sparkly, but they were red and shiny, and that was perfect for me.

As the years went by, shoes weren't my life, but I noticed them. Early on in my life, I decided that I wanted to be a teacher. I just knew it was my purpose in life. I watched my teachers and my play almost always included my practicing what I had observed from them. I noticed that the teachers who really made an impact mostly wore shoes that were comfortable. I know now that this was probably because standing for most of the day in a classroom takes a toll on the feet. I believe that the teachers who I had really admired were focused on reaching the kids in their classroom. They wanted learning to be fun, and it is hard to make things fun if your focus is on your tired and aching feet.

There were other teachers, of course, who didn't wear comfortable shoes. I had a few teachers who wore heels daily. Some of them could really pull it off, and they seemed comfortable in their super cute shoes. They still made learning fun, but they were few and far between.

Then there were yet other teachers who wore cute shoes, but you could just tell that their focus wasn't completely on teaching. You could just see that their feet were killing them. They didn't walk around the classroom. If you needed assistance, you were going to have to make the trek up to their desk. You could even sometimes see that they had kicked off those shoes and were letting their feet rest under their desk.

I am sure you are wondering what shoes have to do with living your purpose. It is a bit of a leap, I suppose, but trust me. Hear me out.

I chose, fairly early on in life, to wear comfortable shoes. I wanted to be able to focus on my purpose. Those teachers who made the greatest impact on me had done what was necessary to make fulfilling their purpose as enjoyable as possible. Their focus was on putting all of their energy into their passion.

I didn't end up being a teacher, in the traditional sense of the word, but I did find that my calling has always been service-oriented. You will find me in comfortable shoes a majority of the time. I am then able to more fully focus on doing what I am doing.

I had this all figured out. I was living my purpose. I had a job, had actually had several jobs, which were service focused. I was helping others. I was getting paid to do it. I thought, "I have the hang of this 'living your purpose' thing!" I spent time in several fields, each of them helping someone in some way.

I spent time working in a youth shelter and then a youth detention center. I loved talking with the youth and listening to their stories, praising them for being strong and courageous. I listened to the youth in detention and heard their stories, and encouraged them not to let a mistake or two determine how they viewed themselves.

I spent time at a residential youth drug and alcohol treatment center and was able to be someone to listen to their stories without judgment and to encourage them to follow their dreams, letting them know that no matter what the past held, it didn't have to hold them back.

I spent time at a middle school and was able to help eighth graders find themselves and learn to be who they truly were. I spent much of my time with the eighth graders who were in trouble as the In School Suspension Supervisor. I spent a good amount of time teaching students methods to calm themselves down and to learn to make better choices.

I spent time at a child advocacy center where I got to help caregivers and parents learn how to deal with the aftermath of abuse of a child. We dealt mainly with sexual abuse cases, but also had physical abuse, neglect and witness-to-violence cases. I heard heart-wrenching stories and was able to help the parents and children to cope.

I have been very blessed in finding and keeping employment which allowed me to serve others. Every time I was able to help another, it blessed me in ways that I am still only beginning to understand. Every experience has been a helpful piece of my journey, and I felt with every ounce of my being that I had been living my purpose.

Imagine how my world crumbled when at one of those jobs, my employer began to ask me to do things that didn't align with my moral compass. How was I going to live my purpose without that job? How was I going to live my purpose with the job if I felt morally corrupt?

What if I had been wrong about "living my purpose"? Could that even be possible? I thought that I *was* living my purpose. Why would the universe snatch that away from me?

I lived in anguish over this for quite some time. How is it that I was suppose to live with myself in this job where I had been serving and helping people, but now felt as if the things I was being asked to do would actually detract from helping our clients. I was completely out of alignment. I began searching for another job, one that would let me continue feeling purposeful in life.

My job search was getting nowhere, and I was feeling more and more lost. I began to give less energy to my job. I started looking for purpose elsewhere. I spent more time with my friends and other social gatherings. I heard other people feeling lost and without direction.

I began talking with the other people that I ran across who had lost their direction. I asked them probing questions. I helped them to find their direction. It is amazing what helping others can do to help yourself. I felt like I might be doing something that fulfilled my purpose again.

I began really working with people, coaching them in finding what brings them joy. I began teaching classes and hosting workshops that focused on finding joy in the present moment. It was back! My purpose had been restored. I was living with joy once again. I found that, much like every other experience in my life, I had learned an extremely valuable lesson. I am here to tell you that I have found that shoes have made all the difference.

I am sure by this point you are asking yourself, "What is this woman talking about? How does that have anything to do with shoes?" I know. I would be confused, too.

I was wearing comfortable shoes, in a manner of speaking, doing what felt good, right and comfortable. All of the sudden, I was made to wear shoes that I didn't want to wear. I was uncomfortable and unhappy. I became focused on the discomfort rather than my purpose. It distracted me from love and joy. I tried on some new shoes. I kept trying on new shoes until I found what was comfortable and allowed me to enjoy love and joy again.

I found my shiny red patent leather shoes – the shoes that allowed me to live my purpose.

I try to wear my comfortable shoes all the time. They allow me to focus on my purpose. They may not actually be little red patent leather Mary Janes, but they remind me to stay in the flow, to trust my instincts and do what feels good and right.

Now I know that purpose doesn't come in the form of a job – although it is wonderful when a job fits in with your purpose – it comes from living from a centered place which allows your joy to flow.

You want to live your purpose? Great! Find what brings you joy. Do it. Make it a part of your daily activities. It doesn't matter what you do for a job, bring your joy to your work, whatever it is. Incorporate what you love into your life.

You know, it is funny. I can almost hear Glenda, the Good Witch of *The Wizard of Oz* fame telling me that I had the power all along; I just had to figure it out for myself. You do, too, you know. You have the power. There is a lot to be said about a pair of red shoes.

Dedicated to Lydia and Gage - I am always amazed at the wonderful things you teach me.

Special thanks to all of the many teachers in my life and to those from whom I continue to learn daily. In particular, I would like to thank my Healing Sisters – Kara, Santalena, Emily, Jade, Krissy, Nori and Jan. You make my world a wonderful and nurturing place. I love you.

~ Shellie Couch

You will recognize your own path when you come upon it because you will suddenly have all the energy and imagination you will ever need.

~ ZIG ZIGLAR

Sandra J. Filer

SANDRA J. FILER, MBA, is a gifted artist, speaker, author, beauty consultant, and licensed Heal Your Life® Coach & Workshop Leader, Sandra is also actively involved with the Woman Within Organization and the Empowered Girls Alliance. She is passionate about empowering people to live happy, healthy, and love-filled lives through coaching and workshops.

Sandra lives on a quiet lantern lit street with her love, Mr. Kim Coffman, and six fabulous felines. She enjoys her family, friends, having fun, creating art, being in nature, and escaping to her favorite island in Florida.

diosafeliz@hotmail.com
www.thehappygoddess.com

🌸 Thomas the Teaching Tom Cat

> God made the cat in order that man might have
> the pleasure of caressing the lion.
>
> ~ FERNAND MERY

On a quiet, lantern-lit street, in the big bustling city of Houston, a striped tom cat lives on a condo porch. He has been lovingly named Thomas. Why he has chosen *our* particular building, on a street full of condominiums and apartments with porches, I can only guess. The story that I make up about it is that somewhere underneath his fraying coat, he knew that he would receive love, which he does. In addition to receiving love, Thomas also gives love.

He has also been a great teacher. Just recently, he gave me the opportunity to really see my life purpose in action. This purpose is to be of loving service.

When I was a very small child, my mother would sit me down with a little plastic record player, turn it on for me, and I would sit by that record player listening to music for hours. One of my favorite stories of all was "The Ugly Duckling." My mom shared that it always intrigued her that as such a small, small child, I would cry whenever I listened to that record. Her summation was that I was a very tender-hearted child. As it turns out, I am also a very tender-hearted adult, and it is all a very special part of my life's purpose.

Thomas the tom cat is a castaway. I guess you might say that he was someone's ugly duckling. At one time, as the story goes, he was a beloved pet … and then he got left behind. I can relate to this. Maybe this is why I have a tender spot for Thomas and other animals tossed out by their owners to live on their own.

Over the years, Thomas and I have developed a special bond. Each morning I shuffle down my hallway with his bowl of food. When I reach the porch, he is either right there ready to greet me, or he is perched on my window ledge waiting for his meal. If it is the latter of the two, I only have to yell out his name, and he comes running. Actually, it is sort of like a cat gallop.

On really special days, he gets a handful of diced ham snagged from the salad bar at lunch. He loves that! Each day I refill his water bowl, check to make sure that his bedding is comfortable, and I make the time to pet him and let him know that he is loved.

This relationship is reciprocal. You see, each time that I pull up in front of our building, much like a dog, Thomas comes running off the porch, over the esplanade, and into the street to greet me as I open my car door. It fills my heart to be so loved.

Recently, Thomas developed an infection on his nose. Immediately, I took action. I began treating it with an ointment. I found myself completely consumed with wanting him to be well. I'd visit him on the porch 3-4 times a day. I'd take him treats. I'd put ointment on his nose each and every visit.

One night, I met a new resident in the hallway. She asked me if I was caring for "that cat on the patio." I assured her that I was, and he was on the mend. She turned and looked at me and said, "That is so awesome. He is the reason that I choose to live here." This really intrigued me. She then proceeded to say, "When I saw Thomas on the porch the day I looked at my unit, I thought to myself, I want to live where people care for animals and allow them on the porch." Wow! This really touched me deeply. Not only because of the impact Thomas had made on this resident but also because I knew that I was the one caring for him, and until then, I had no idea that my caring had such an impact on someone else.

On another occasion, I was exiting my back door to cross paths with yet another resident. In my hand was a can of cat food. He looked at me and with a smile across his face asked, "Are you the one taking care of Thomas?" This was followed up with, "What is wrong with his nose?" My excited reply was something along the lines of, "Doesn't he look 90 percent better?" My neighbor then shared, "That is so wonderful. God is going to bless you even more for what you do." I closed the door. Again, wow! I had no idea that so many people were paying attention.

Yet, I was one of the only ones taking action. Something began to stir inside of me. As a result of all the dealings with Thomas, I began to really take a look at myself and my life. The question that surfaced for me is: Why am I the one who is taking action? Why am I the one that feels so passionate about helping an abandoned animal? After all, it isn't just Thomas that I feed. My patio seems to be a magnet for all of those furry castaways.

One awareness after another began to enter into my consciousness. I realized first of all that Thomas was on our building's porch because I was meant to learn from him. The first lesson that I learned was that one doesn't have to "do" anything to serve a purpose.

This was big for me. I have been the person who equates my worthiness or purpose with the amount of money I do or do not make. Whether or not I am truly serving my purpose has been measured by the number of participants in a workshop. Not necessarily "what" the participants got from the workshop. When I heard the neighbor share that having Thomas on the patio was her reason for choosing her residence, I had one of the "aha" moments. Thomas was simply being himself. Thomas was being a cat.

Taking this a step further, I had lunch with a friend. During the lunch, we were catching up on life. We've been friends for 13 years. Over the years we have each done a lot of personal growth work. We shared stories after stories. She was embarking upon a transition with her job. As the conversation continued, she looked at me and said, "Diosa .. You have no idea the impact you have had on my life." I leaned a little more forward as I listened.

She went on to say, "Remember the time that you said to me, 'Marie, you deserve a man with two legs of the same size and a head with hair.'" I sat sort of stunned. The memory did not surface for me. She elaborated, "The point was that I deserved someone 'better,' it really wasn't about the legs or the hair, it was about the man that he wasn't. I was playing with the turkeys instead of the eagles." Again, I sat there and listened. She said, "That feedback from you shifted my life."

My eyes welled up with tears and again, I thought of Thomas. He just sits there on the porch and has an impact. I apparently just sat at that infamous lunch sharing from my tender-hearted self and made a difference.

It is amazing what happens in the Universe when one ponders such a thing as purpose. Life begins to bring example after example. This is because oftentimes, we need to be given multiple examples for it to truly settle in. At yet another lunch, I sat next to sweet little Gabriella.

She is five years old. As the conversation ensued, she said, "Tia you are my rainbow." Her rainbow? Again, the tears welled up in my eyes. What was happening here?

The power in *that* example is that not too long ago, I was literally in tears because I didn't feel like I was "enough." As usual, I was measuring my worthiness by the number of participants or the lack thereof. As I sat on my pity pot, I cried and said to my husband, "I might as well change my email signature to say: good friend." He consoled me in his own way and assured me that I was enough and that I was exactly where I needed to be. Of course, he was absolutely right. I was and I am exactly where I need to be.

Purpose seems to be something that so many of us are searching to find. For years, I earned title after title believing I was on purpose. Over time, I saw that I was reaching for one accomplishment after another believing I was living my purpose.

However, in caring for Thomas' nose on the front porch, it finally really became clear to me. Doting on him and mending his boo boos felt right. Sharing lunch with my friend and listening to her share our past and how it has affected her future felt right. Being Gabriella's rainbow felt right. It all felt really good at the level of the soul, and I felt fulfilled, enriched, loved, and ultimately, filled with purpose.

Who knew that a striped tom cat living on a porch could be such a great teacher? I believe that Thomas' example is a testimonial to the fact that we are each here to be exactly who we are and *that* is our purpose. We are here to live fully. We are here to receive love and to give love.

I am grateful to have Thomas in my life. I am grateful to be given the opportunity to love him and receive love in return.

So often we make things far more difficult than they actually need to be. We search and search and look outside of ourselves. In reality we come fully equipped to live our purpose. All we need to do is open our eyes and hearts to the experience. It is a matter of embracing it!

Now I ask you, what is *your* purpose?

Did you hear it? If not, I invite you to allow the answer to come to you in the whisper of the wind. Or, maybe it will come when a stranger enters your path. All I know is that whether you believe it or not, you are someone's rainbow, too.

How could life be any more beautiful than that? What greater purpose than to be known as the one who "cares" or puts color into another's life.

Yes, my purpose is to be of service … Now, onto more rainbow moments.

This story is dedicated to everyone out there wondering if they are enough. You are.

First of all, I wish to thank Thomas. Also for everyone (and anyone) who stopped to pet him, provide water, and/or rearrange his fleece blanket, thank you. I wish to express my extreme gratitude to the animal control employee who released Thomas, when his "job" was to do otherwise. Without my sister sending antibiotics and my neighbor Eric's assistance, Thomas would not be here today ... so I thank them both, from the bottom of my heart! Finally, I thank my feline-loving editor, Dr. Denise Coleman, for lovingly assisting with the purr-fect adjustments to the story.

~ Sandra J. Filer

Alan Michael

ALAN MICHAEL is an innovative Graphic Designer and owns and operates Alan Michael Design. He is a gifted animal communicator, psychic reader, seer of past lives, and energy healer. Alan is passionate about sharing his gifts and experiences with people to help awaken their gifts so they can create the life they dream.

Alan lives in Edina, MN where he enjoys spending time with soul friends and family, his two rescue dogs, playing guitar, writing music, gardening, cooking, home remodeling, traveling and the outdoors.

alan@alanmichael.com

❧ Be My Strength

"Wake up Uncle Al, something terrible has happened," my 26 year old nephew said, as he shook me from a sound sleep. "What are you talking about?" I replied. "Grandpa died, your Dad … the family has been trying to call us all morning. We have to get over to your parent's apartment right away." Half asleep and stunned, I crawled out of bed. My nephew was pacing in the living room and said, "I knew something bad was going to happen today, I told you … it's all my fault, I should have done something." I consoled my nephew, "That's not yours. You had nothing to do with this, and it's not your fault. It was Dad's time, his decision and choice he made a long time ago, before he came to earth."

The night before, my nephew and I had stayed up late talking. He told me he had a dream or premonition and couldn't figure out the message. Within a few weeks or a few months he usually understands the meaning. Before we went to sleep, he said, "I'm telling you Uncle Al, something either really good or really bad is going to happen tomorrow when we wake up, I have a really bad feeling." I replied, "There is nothing to fear. It's an intuitive gift you have from God. It's Spirit sending you a message to help you see what is coming up in your life and to help you make decisions."

I called my brother. "What happened?" I asked. "Mom said, 'Dad was not feeling well lately and could not sleep and was up four to five times during the night.' She was not sure if he was dreaming, talking to her, his Angels or his Mother who had passed, but she heard Dad say, 'I'm not ready to go yet.' He got up and went into the bathroom. Dad called for her, and as she entered the bathroom, she saw his knees buckle, and he fell and hit his head on the bathtub. He was still breathing, and she went to the kitchen and called 911. While still on the phone, she saw he was not breathing anymore. The paramedics were never able to get a pulse from him." My brother said, "The whole family is here. If you want to see Dad before the funeral home picks up his body in an hour, you should get over here right away ... I will stall them as much as I can." "We're on our way," I replied. I walked into the bathroom and splashed cold water on my face. I starred at myself in the mirror and said, "Now what do we do?"

As my nephew and I drove to my parent's home, I asked the Angels to surround us and give the family strength. My nephew and I walked into my parent's apartment. I felt present and aware of everything going on in the room. I could feel the heaviness of hearts and emotions. One by one, I hugged each of my siblings, my mother and aunt, my uncle and cousin. I placed my hand on each person's chest and asked, "How's your heart?"

My brother said, "Dad's in the bedroom if you want to see him." I walked down the hall and into the bedroom. Several sisters were in the room. Some were standing, others sitting on the bed, and some were kneeling beside him saying goodbye. I knelt down beside my Father. An intubation tube was in his mouth. I placed my hands on his chest and wept. I said, "Oh Pops, what happened? ... You wore yourself out." I felt hands on my shoulder. I turned to see my brother. Kneeling at my Father's head, I placed my hands on his chest. I wanted to see if I could feel any life energy from him, but I could not. I held his face and kissed his cheeks and forehead for the last time. I could not feel him when I held his body. I thought I could lightly feel his presence in the room behind us on the other side of the bed.

I stood up and hugged my brother with our father laying on the floor directly below our feet. While embracing my brother, a vivid color image appeared in my mind of a lit Medieval Torch being handed to me. The image then projected from my mind, outside my forehead directly in front of my eyes. I heard my Father say, "Be my strength. You children look after one another, be kind to one another, love one another." I shared Dad's words with my siblings as tears streamed down their faces. But I kept to myself the image of the lit torch and "Be my strength" for a few days.

The family stood together holding hands in a prayer circle around Dad. I asked my Mother if she wanted to say anything, and she quietly said, "No." I began to speak, and the words flowed through me. I was being guided. There were experiences and feelings Dad had shared with me, that I knew would be healing to my family's hearts. "Dad, you were a Warrior and one of my greatest and toughest teachers. I love you and thank you for everything."

I shared a story of one of the last times I played golf with Dad, on Father's Day several years back. "It was a beautiful blue sky morning, just like today," I said. "Dad and I were outside on my patio, and I gave him a Father's Day card. Inside the card I thanked him for being a great father, a friend and one of my greatest and toughest teachers." I expressed, "We had been through a lot of good times and tough times together, and I was proud of him and to be his son. That much of what he taught me had helped me be the man I am today and continue to try and embody. As my father read the card, tears streamed down his face. He looked at me, and said, 'I can't tell you how much I appreciate what you wrote … how much those words mean to me. I have struggled as a father and a man, with choices I have made, what I could have done differently. God spoke to me, Al, and he told me to look after those children … and I did … Ma and I did the best we could.' Then he gave me one of the best long hugs of my life, and he kissed me on my cheek.

"We went golfing and the course was not very busy. We took our time and hit extra shots. There were geese on the course that Dad enjoyed. I stopped the cart and picked up several goose feathers and gave him one. Dad smiled. As we approached a green, we saw a Mama Mallard duck and her baby ducklings swimming in the water. Dad said, 'Look at how beautiful they are, and the way the light is shining on them. She's a proud Mama, look how she's showing them off. She's doing her job!'"

My cousin spoke with tears streaming down his face. "I didn't have a dad growing up, your dad was my dad. I want to thank your family for sharing your dad with me and my family. Charlie was tops in my book, and I always knew how your Dad felt about me and our love for one another."

My brother told of a time while talking to Dad and was sharing some tough times he was going through in his marriage, raising two young kids, a career and finances. Dad caringly replied, "I don't know how you do it, Son. Everything you're going through, that's a lot." My brother said, "Are you kidding me? It's nothing compared to what you and Mom went through raising nine kids and working two to three jobs at a time. Where do you think I learned perseverance?"

Shortly after our prayer circle concluded, the funeral home attendants arrived to take Dad away. My brother ushered the family away from the bedroom, hall and kitchen away from view of them placing Dad on the gurney. While standing in the kitchen, facing the hallway, I watch the two attendants, one in front and one in back, wheel my Father down the hall toward the apartment door. I saw my Father, in his blue pajamas, following and observing himself being wheeled away. I heard my Father say, "That's a helluva contraption they have there." I looked at my brother and said, "Did you see that?" He replied, "I didn't see it, but I believe you."

In the parking lot saying goodbye to my family, I express I am really interested to see how Dad shows himself to us all. "Watch for signs and messages from him. Dad was such a creative guy and loved nature and music. I'm curious what kind of signs he will show us."

I drove home and was warmly greeted by my three rescue dogs, my family. I was not home long when I hear a thrashing sound coming from my dining room. Flutter, flutter, bang, bang, against the patio glass door. I walk to the dining room and see it is a male robin. The robin lands and perches on the wrought iron chair just inches outside my patio door and stares at me. I'm thinking, okay, it is spring and mating season, and the males are territorial, and the patio glass is like a mirror. Then I remember, on Saturday morning, the day before my Father's passing, my nephew had complained about a noise that woke him up. While I was still in bed, my nephew shouted, "What is all the racket? … something has been banging on that patio door window all morning long!" I get out of bed and open the patio door blinds, and there is a male robin fluttering and banging against the glass, then perches on the top backside of a wrought iron chair sitting outside my patio door, just inches away. That male robin had sat and stared at me, too. Now, I begin to wonder, was that some type of sign foreshadowing my father's death?

The next day, I awoke and walk from my bedroom to the living room. Once again, the noise at the patio glass door. I open the blinds and there he is, Mr. Robin. Once again, he perches on the top backside of the wrought iron chair sitting outside my patio door, and stares at me! Now this is starting to feel like a sign, but I'm still not sure. I make coffee and let the dogs out. I am in my home office sitting at my desk in front of my computer. I'm thinking about my Dad and everything that has transpired in the last 24 hours.

Suddenly, the song, "Somewhere Over The Rainbow," pops into my mind, and I begin singing the song. It was one of my parents' favorite songs. As a family we watched *The Wizard of Oz* so many times together. The movie came out in 1936, and that was the year my Mom was born. I think of the late, great Hawaiian, Israel "IZ," who sings and plays a beautiful Ukulele version of that song mixed with "It's a Wonderful World," by Louis Armstrong. I find the music video on YouTube and begin to watch and listen and sing along. I am thinking I want to learn to play this song on the Ukulele and perform at my Dad's Life Celebration. Less than a minute into the song, I hear this thrashing against my home office window just a few feet away. I turn to look and there sits the male robin in my flower box outside my window. I burst into tears, and say, "I love you, Dad."

My Father loved nature and animals. He marveled and respected their beauty, purity and cheery personality. He sang a song about robins to us kids when we were young. He and Mom had robins and other bird plates, painted eggs and toys in their china hutch at home. As a child the robins would nest and have their babies in the Pine tree outside our kitchen window. Our family would watch the robin family as we ate our meals. A few of the Totem messages and symbolism of the Robin are: growth, renewal, spring, rebirth of spirit, the power of song and joy in your heart, clarity, new beginnings and a bright future.

The robin appeared daily, inside my windowsill two feet away, close enough to pet. One day the robin perched on top of my car, then the windshield wiper, then flew and landed on my windowsill. The Messenger would appear to lift my Spirits at key moments when I was deep in thought preparing for my Father's Service and particularly when I would become overwhelmed with emotion. My oldest sister suggested I open the window before the little feller hurt himself. I opened my office window and the screen completely. I began writing down what a friend told me minutes earlier on the phone: "If you can step outside your grief and be present, the signs are everywhere." The moment I finished writing those words, I hear a flutter to my right. I turned my head slowly, and there sitting inside my open window, inside the windowsill was the robin two feet away. I was thrilled!

I was happy to share my experiences with family and friends via e-mail, text, phone calls and on Facebook. Friends expressed how much they appreciated that I was sharing these messages and the whole experience. They began sharing messages they received of loved ones crossed. The love and support from friends and family was incredible and healing to my heart. My family, too, was excited and comforted. My siblings also experienced profound signs from Dad in nature, from animals, birds, his presence while praying, in dreams and heard his whispers.

My Father died on Easter and his Life Celebration was on April 14th, my Birthday. He was a clever guy. On Facebook I wrote, "It's my 51st Birthday, it's my Father's Life Celebration and the weather could not be more perfect. Dad's been with me all morning. This is a Great Day of Love and Celebrating, and I am excited! Wish me luck today as I speak in honor of my Father and my Family. I will make you proud Paw!"

The seating room, hallway and back room were filled at my Father's Life Celebration. As I saw the room fill with people from all time periods of my Father's life, my life, my family's life ... it was like watching souls from a life's play, come back on stage. Each person had their role, had their part in this play of life. During my speech I felt clear, present, powerful and full of love and emotion. I spoke from the heart. I know I had help from my Father and my Angels. There was not a dry eye in the house, and there was also lots of laughter and many moments of inspiration and hope.

My father wanted everyone to know, he had a GREAT life. He chose a challenging life and made choices for tremendous soul growth. He tried to make amends before he left. He knows he held grudges too long. He had a difficult time expressing his feelings and saying he was sorry, and he didn't like to rehash things. He said he was sorry with a smile, a big bear hug, a kiss and I love you. He's telling me to tell everyone to make amends faster. Let bygones be bygones. Water under the bridge. Too much time wasted. Your time together is precious. It goes by so fast. Enjoy and create the good times. Blood is blood, but etherically, we are all Soul family. Through his eyes, through each of his children and their family, he sees himself and his life dreams really did come true.

My father handed me the lit torch; however, I am just the messenger. The torch and his message, "Be my Strength," are for his nine children who he loves forever and with all his heart. And as I type these words, goose bumps radiate my body in validation, and I see him smiling, nodding, "Yes."

Dedicated to my father, Charles Louis Weleczki, for your love and continuing to be one of my greatest teachers. Thank you for this beautiful experience that I can share with the world, in hopes of healing hearts and shining a light on everyone's God-given gifts. I love you, Dad!

To God for your love, this life and giving me so much.

To my loving mother Suzanne, for teaching me to be kind, positive and see the good in people. To my brother and seven sisters for their love, friendship, choosing me as their family and being my teachers. To my animal soul family Louie, CooterBear, HoJo and Dodge who loved me unconditionally and taught me how to laugh, play, trust and love again. To Sunny Dawn, for your friendship, being my teacher, seeing my gifts and always supporting and encouraging my spiritual path with love. I love you all.

~ Alan Michael

Kim Pratte

KIMBERLY PRATTE resides in Milwaukee, WI, where she has recently opened her own private practice, and is studying at the School of Integrative Spiritual Psychology and at Blue Sky School of Professional Massage & Therapeutic Bodywork.

Kimberly is a co-author of two books and feels that her writing is in response to her life experiences. Her passion is to assist others along their journey of healing and self-discovery through sharing her own life experiences and the tools she has found to be beneficial in creating the life she has always dreamed of.

kimpratte@gmail.com
www.kimberlypratte.com

🌸 Spiritual Path to Life Success

For most of my life, my purpose wasn't clear to me. I was a wife and a mother who was constantly taking care of others and meeting their needs. I didn't know how to care for myself and felt there had to be more to this life. Through the many shifts and changes I have experienced in my life, I found myself on a spiritual path to life success and realized we as humans aren't defined by what we do, rather by how we choose to live our lives. We are more prepared to take care of others if we first take care of ourselves.

This past year has been one of transition for me; one that has completely transformed my perception of myself and who I thought I was. I became a grandmother, moved, became a published author, found myself in an empty nest, and lost a significant relationship. Through all of this, I have learned how to care for myself instead of constantly focusing on everyone else's needs. After going through a very difficult breakup in December of 2011, I simply felt as if I couldn't even breathe; much less make it through the day.

By applying the following techniques I learned how to calm my mind and focus on the present moment. Through this process I also started realizing what it meant for me to live my purpose. This required transitioning my thought process and way of living. I felt I was living my purpose by being a mother and focusing on taking care of others. While that may be partially true, some very important pieces were missing. Those pieces were practicing daily self-care and learning how to stay in the present moment.

At one point in January, I had to shut myself off from most people. I was unable to reach out to others or to receive what they had to offer. I had to stay with me in order to work through some very difficult emotions. I could not take on more issues from the outside or be accountable for scheduled meetings and conversations. I found the external distractions were creating stress for me which was clouding the core work I needed to do within myself. I didn't know how to verbalize this. I don't think I could because I really didn't know what was going on with me at the time. I just shut down. I feel this was an important first step in the learning process of how to take care of myself and put my needs first. I felt selfish, but it was a necessary step for me to become whole again.

One key component to overall spiritual growth and development is through integrating the mind, body, and spirit connection. Through this you become balanced and whole. If you neglect one or more, you become unbalanced and your body will be in a state of dis-ease. I began a daily practice of meditation, walks, proper rest, and nutrition. I quickly noticed I was feeling much better physically, and had a much better outlook mentally. No longer did I look at experiences as being good or bad, instead I was grateful for the lessons and opportunities for growth. While we may not realize it at the time we are in the midst of a situation, all of our experiences are opportunities for learning and growth.

In February, I started attending the T'ai Chi Ch'uan Center of Milwaukee. T'ai Chi is form of martial arts and an excellent daily practice for relaxation, meditation, self-defense, and generally increasing your health. I continue to develop my understanding of this exercise, and further integrate my mind, body, and spirit in order to create more balance in my life.

My connection, not only with Spirit but also with myself, has increased exponentially. I'm much more balanced and centered within myself. I feel more in tune to my purpose as I continue on the path toward living the life I have always wanted and am intended to live. Doors are opening as if a spiritual pathway is being cleared to assist me in reaching my goals. I sit quietly and tune into my own inner thoughts as I seek guidance in everything I do. My spirit of laughter and joy has come back into focus, I have found me again, and within that is my life purpose.

Several things recently presented themselves as evidence I have reached my desired outcome, and I will touch on two of them. First, my daughter came to visit me in March and asked me, "What did you do with my mother?" She immediately recognized I had become much happier, more relaxed and was my light-hearted self again. She was delighted with the changes. We shared heartfelt laughter over her statement and discussed all of the changes I made within myself and in my surroundings.

Secondly, my younger brother recently told me he hasn't seen me like this since I was seventeen years old, again for the same reasons my daughter recognized. Coming from my little brother this was a powerful statement of observation. We talked about how I had gotten so far away from my true self and my journey back to me. People and opportunities are presenting themselves, enabling me to create and live a more purposeful life as I tap into the gifts I have to offer.

I recently heard Frank Sinatra sing "You're Nobody 'Til Somebody Loves You." I feel this is so untrue. You're nobody until you find, or come into yourself by fully understanding and knowing who you are. Until you fully appreciate and respect yourself, your spiritual gifts, and your talents, you aren't capable of fully loving yourself, much less loving others. No one can do this for you. Until you're able to achieve this love for yourself you're just a shell living a lie in the shadow of a life you "think" you should be living. I don't know about you, but I don't want to be defined by whether or not I'm loved by another, but rather whether or not I love myself, what I'm doing with my life and how I impact the lives of others.

The Evolution of Change

In the beginning I needed to focus more on the connected breath, meditation, learning how to let go of the hurt, and how to live my life in the present moment by just allowing things to be what they are. I had to learn to trust, stay in the present moment, and how to live my dreams.

My focus shifted to a place of living my life with more gratitude and truly listening to my inner voice and guides, not just disregarding these things and focusing on what I thought everyone else wanted me to do. I learned to trust more fully in the universe and my needs being provided for as I remain in the present moment. I no longer create drama in my life by worrying about what happened yesterday and what is to come tomorrow. I accept that everything is and will be as it should. I have changed the way I view my past hurts, recognizing and having gratitude for the lessons. Without those lessons I would not be where I am today. When I feel myself getting off track, I simply take time for myself. This could be a simple contemplative meditative walk as I focus on taking deep and clearing breaths and listen for the truths being revealed to me. The results are phenomenal.

Taking time to expand my knowledge, try new things, and explore my creativity have all been key components to my recent evolution. By walking outside of my comfort zone I became an author, attended a drum building class, and am now pursuing school to become a Professional Massage Therapist/Therapeutic Body Worker. Becoming a massage therapist is part of living my purpose and my desire to help others, especially those who are terminally ill or recovering from surgery or injury. There are actually people out there that the only touch they get is from massage. I find this to be very sad and disturbing, everyone needs human touch.

Change is always present for all of us, and reaching out to grow in new ways brings about healthy improvements on our spiritual path to life success. Everything that we are, our thoughts, our feelings and our beliefs, they are all an integral part of living our purpose.

 Yesterday I was clever, so I wanted to change the world. Today I am wise, so I am changing myself.

~ JALAL AD-DIN RUMI

Discoveries

After going through the break-up in December, I realized how far off track I was from living my life fully and enjoying things I'm interested in. I had been living in fear and for everyone else. I wasn't taking care of myself emotionally or spiritually. The biggest thing for me was learning how to live alone and be alone. The interesting thing is how, in the blink of an eye, I went from always being with others and caring for them, to suddenly living alone, being alone, and even working entirely alone in the office. I had never experienced this level of aloneness. I went straight from my parent's house to being married and having children. The solitude has been crucial to my learning. I now realize I'm not alone at all, even when I'm alone.

Throughout my youth I used to intentionally close myself up in my room, hide in the corner of my closet, crawl out on the roof of the house, or seek refuge in the woods sitting by a stream in order to be alone and contemplate life. Once I married, I found this type of solace in my nature hikes with the kids and trips to the mountains hiking and camping. Since the year 2000 I had lost my connection to this insightful time I found so important. I'm grateful to be reconnected with this practice. I'm also back to my light-hearted nature where I find joy in the simplest of things and readily laugh at situations.

I'm embracing my relationship with my parents and reconnecting with my younger brother. I'm remembering life doesn't have to be a challenge or lived fearfully. I have realized just how immensely important being out in nature and appreciating animals is to me; it nourishes me and renews my spirit. In order to truly be happy and have joy in my life I need to be in touch with myself, that kind of joy is truly contagious. We all need to find the joy in our life, and use it.

I have completely transformed not only my daily activities, but my thought process, or way of thinking as well, which enables me to live a more spirit-filled life of purpose. I now devote every day to living my purpose. Some days are better than others, but that is part of the process of change. As I continue my journey down the spiritual path to life success, I realize my purpose is to be me, and to be open to opportunities for growth and change.

 What counts in life is not the mere fact that we have lived. It is what difference we have made to the lives of others that will determine the significance of the life we lead.

~ NELSON MANDELA

Insights

Following are some affirmations I came across that really sum up what I have embraced more deeply during my journey along the spiritual path to life success this past year which I would like to share with you.

Courage

I am the beloved of God. I am supported and guided in all that I do. Knowing this, I have the courage to pursue my heart's desires with the confidence that all is well.

Grace

I am the love of God. I surrender to my highest good now. My life is lived in grace. I live my life from grace. For this knowing, I am grateful.

Clarity

I am tapped into the mind of God. Therefore, I experience only clarity in all situations. I am the clear emanation of God.

Love

I stand in the knowing that love is all there is. Love is the source of all life. Love is the source of my being. I radiate love wherever I go. I am the love of God.

~ UNKNOWN

This chapter is dedicated to those seeking their purpose, may you find inspiration within these pages. Never give up on your dreams and passions, for these are the foundation for living your purpose.

Thank you to my family and friends for your encouragement, love, and support. I couldn't do the things I do with you!!

~ Kim Pratte

There is no greater gift
you can give or receive
than to honor your calling.
It's why you were born.
And how you become
most truly alive.

~ OPRAH WINFREY

Jody Kratz

JODY KRATZ RN, BSN has been in the healing arts for more than 20 years. She has blended her vast experience into a unique heart-centered approach to help people transform their lives. She started out as a Heal Your Life® teacher and Coach and became a certified Calling in the One coach to focus on helping people attract their soul mate. Jody is also a sixth sensory practitioner certified by Sonia Choquette. She blends her intuition with her transformative coaching to help people realize their dreams. Jody is also an author, public speaker, and a facilitator for The Wish® game.

jody@innerlifeinvestments.com
www.innerlifeinvestments.com

Live Your Joy

> When you do things from your soul, you feel a
> river moving in you, a joy.
>
> ~ RUMI

Living your joy is the path to your purpose. It is a winding path full of loops and turns, and you never know what lies beyond the next bend. The path is full of choices that either bring you more in line with your purpose or leave you lost in confusion. Luckily there are many signs along the way – all you need to do is recognize them and follow. There are Angels with you to help you along the way just waiting for you to ask for their guidance. You will run into people along the path who want to guide you, and many of them are loved ones who are trying to help and protect you.

Have you ever stopped to think what really makes you happy? We tend to compartmentalize our lives and justify unhappiness in one area by telling ourselves that we can't have it all. There was a time in my life when I loved my job and my kids, but was not happy in my marriage. I figured I was lucky just to have "some" happiness. I realize now that you can have happiness in every area of your life, and there is no need to settle for anything less. In fact, we were brought into this life to find happiness and share it with everyone we meet. Part of finding happiness is to be who you are, not what others expect you to be.

I am a nurse, and I used to work with a patient care technician named Jerry. We worked together for 23 years. I can remember at the beginning of my career seeing Jerry waiting in the hall for a patient who was in a room for testing. He would sit outside the room in a yoga position with his eyes closed and meditate. I witnessed this several times over the years and would always think, "How odd," and go about my business. He always seemed at peace and had a certain serenity about him. The patients loved him.

As the years went by, I ended up being the Nursing Supervisor for the entire hospital, and Jerry was still a patient care technician. I always wondered, "Why doesn't he go to nursing school? Doesn't he want to better himself?" I would often tell him that the hospital would pay his nursing school tuition, but he wasn't interested. I was judging him and telling him what he should do, just as people frequently do to each other. But he did not let anyone's opinion sway him.

I realize now he was living his joy and was confident enough not to care what anyone else thought. He touched so many lives in countless ways with his happiness and serenity. Everyone's purpose is different, and as Jerry proves, it doesn't have to be bigger than life, it just has to bring you true happiness which can be shared with others. He was in touch with his inner guidance and not influenced by external distractions.

Getting in Touch with Your Inner Guidance

 Every time you don't follow your inner guidance, you feel a loss of energy, loss of power, a sense of spiritual sadness.

~ SHAKTI GAWAIN

We all come into this world with an inner guidance system, that little voice inside that tells you: "I don't think you should do that." That little voice you often ignored resulting in disastrous consequences. You can also be guided by higher realms such as angels, religious figures, or spirit guides. Explore the multitude of options and decide what's best for *you*. Whatever form it takes, nurture it and allow it to grow.

The higher realms have unconditional love for you and have only your highest good in mind. I have many different guides and angels, but you have to ask for guidance. They stand by waiting for your invitation because they will never violate your free will. It can take time and practice to really tune in. You can't just ask one time and expect it all to fall into place. It is an ongoing dialogue. It can be confusing at first, but the more you communicate, the clearer the messages will become and the more you will be given. They love when you are excited and grateful for their help.

Ask for signs when you are uncertain. Some people are specific in the sign they ask for such as feathers. I personally like butterflies. Also be on the lookout for synchronicities, and don't chalk it up to merely coincidence. I once had an agonizing decision to make, and while I was on Facebook Debbie Griggs kept popping up. She is a well-known photo psychic and gives awesome readings. I'm thinking to myself, "I just had a reading two weeks ago, why would I do another now?" I convinced myself it was a coincidence and got off Facebook to check my e-mail.

When I opened my e-mail, even though it was on the most current page, in the viewing pane was an old e-mail from Debbie. I thought "This is weird," and kept clicking on new e-mails, but her e-mail continued to come up in the reading pane after I had deleted the one I was reading. I still wasn't getting the message, and must have logged off and logged back in about five times, only to find that e-mail still there. I finally got the hint, scheduled the reading and received the answers I was looking for. It's always your choice if you listen to the guidance or ignore it. You will be provided with many opportunities along your path, but it is up to you to recognize the opportunity and accept it.

I learned the hard way how to discern an opportunity from a test of my commitment from the Universe. The key is to have a clear vision of where you want to be, and when you make a decision, ask yourself if it is consistent with your vision. Your vision and purpose are ever changing and evolving, so you need to sit down once in a while to evaluate where you want to be. A wonderful tool is keeping a journal to have your journey in writing so you can look back and see how far you have come and adjust your purpose and vision when necessary. My vision is to spread love, light, and joy throughout the world. I learned a long time ago not to worry about the "how" and just have faith in the Universe that opportunities would be presented to me. I have had many opportunities over the past few years and made a few mistakes.

My first big opportunity was getting laid off from my job of 23 years. I had been affirming that I had my own business and no longer needed to work at the hospital. I signed up for the Heal Your Life® teacher training before I knew I was going to be laid off. It wasn't exactly what I meant in my affirmation. That training changed my life forever, and when I was laid off, I saw the blessing in it instead of disaster.

I had a six-month severance package with full pay, benefits, and un-employment. I had the time of my life. I trained with Sonia Choquette and also did the Heal Your Life® coach training. I built my own website and hired a business coach. It was one opportunity after another. The six-month severance ended, and I was left with unemployment. I had huge bills to pay because I had been making six figures as a nurse. I hung tough and told everyone I wasn't looking for a job – I didn't care if I lost everything. That was my first mistake. There is no need to lose anything. You get what you think about.

Everyone around me thought they knew what was best for me, and unfortunately I started to listen to the negativity. I was 51 years old and hadn't worked in ten months, who would hire me if I waited any longer? But still, I hung in there. My friend called to tell me of a job opening at the hospital where she was working. I told her I wasn't interested, but in the back of my mind I was thinking that it could pay the bills while I built my business. The Vice President of Nursing called to ask me to come and speak with her. This was unheard of, particularly since I didn't even apply for the job. When I went to meet with her, I learned it was a part-time job, and I accepted. I figured it would help while I got on my feet. What I didn't realize was that it was a test of my commitment to my vision and purpose from the Universe.

I thought the Universe put the job in my lap for a reason so it must be what I'm supposed to do. I never asked myself, "Is this in line with my vision and purpose?" I just blindly thought it was meant to be. Had I thought it through, I would have known it was not in alignment and followed my heart. The job ended up being horrible, and I kept thinking, "Why did the Universe send me this job?" It never dawned on me to just quit, so I looked for another job.

The new job was full time, which meant I was getting further away from my purpose. But since I was able to work from home as a nurse and take phone calls, I convinced myself it was a great job. The Universe did show me some sympathy because the job had a lot of down time which allowed me to work on my business. I even completed another coach training. When the new job asked me to cross-train to letter writing at work, I agreed. Another big mistake. This took away the down time, so now I had no time at all for my business.

I was developing upper back pain and was miserable. I had been being guided for months not to work, and now I was having physical symptoms from not following my heart's desire. It is crucial to stay in tune with your mind, body, and spirit. I realized I couldn't do the job full time any longer, so cut back to two days a week. I justified the decision to myself because it provided needed medical benefits. Two days a week certainly wasn't enough money to live on, but I could go back to working on my business. That lasted about two weeks until the guidance was coming loud and clear to quit the job and have faith. The Universe was testing my commitment to my purpose by having these jobs appear. I realized that even though I thought I had surrendered my life, I really had not.

Surrender

 It all boils down to one thing ... it is your 'relationship' to the source, and that relationship to that which we call God, or don't call God, or don't even know ... is God. It is ALL that really matters ... when you surrender, and stop resisting, and stop trying to change that which you cannot change, but be in the moment, be fully open to the blessings you have already received, and those that are yet to come to you, and stand in that space of gratitude, and honor, and claim that for yourself, and look at where you are, and how far you have come, and what you've gotten, and what you've accomplished, and who you are. When you can claim 'that,' and see that, the literal vibration of your life will change. The Vibration of Your Life Will Change.

~OPRAH WINFREY

I used to pray: "I surrender my life to you, Lord. Please allow me to be a channel for your love and grace." At first, I couldn't even say the word, "surrender." It was very difficult until I finally understood it didn't mean I have to give up my free will. I thought I had surrendered but realized I was only willing to surrender up to a point. That point was financial security. I was living in fear. After decades of working on my inner self, I still was living in fear.

I couldn't make excuses any longer, the time had come. I came to this realization while I was working on this writing project. I'm an intuitive and can hear the messages loud and clear. I now realize that I was not showing my faith in the fact that if I completely surrendered, the Universe would provide me with every opportunity to be successful and prosperous in my vision and purpose. I was scheduled to work yesterday but hadn't finished this chapter yet. So I packed up my equipment, drove into the office and quit on the spot! I have never felt so much freedom and joy. I have finally surrendered to what will be.

I hope that someday our paths may cross, and we can walk together for a while enjoying the present moment without judgment. When you come to a fork in the road remember to ask for insight as to which way is for your highest good. Always know your path is your own, so don't be misled by those who have a different opinion of which turn to take. Only you know which is the right way for you. Follow your heart not your common sense, and you will stay on track. Leave your ego behind and surrender to what the Universe has in store for you. Be grateful for where you are in this moment on your journey and have faith that the best is yet to come.

Always keep your vision and purpose in mind before you act. Be grateful for where you are right now with all that you have, and your life will become more joyful with every step you take. Leave your ego and fear behind, follow your heart, don't worry about what's around the bend, live in the present moment, and enjoy the journey. Live your joy!

🔆 Never regret having chosen or met Wrong People in our life, because NO ONE can teach us right lessons better than Wrong People.

~ TATHAASTU

My chapter is dedicated to the "teachers" who helped me learn the lessons in life I needed to create my beautiful new life.

Special eternal gratitude to my mother, Joanne Shearman, who has always loved and believed in me when no one else did. She is my rock.

~ Jody Kratz

Tammy Gynell Lagoski

TAMMY GYNELL LAGOSKI is a published author, publishing consultant, and is knowledgeable in Grief Coaching and working with diverse populations. She was raised on a farm in Charleston, Illinois and currently resides in Peoria, Illinois, where she enjoys spending time with her husband, daughter, three step daughters, sons-in-law and new grand-baby. She also enjoys spending time with her two dogs, Francie and Molly, who are as rambunctious as a couple of two year olds.

tammylag@gmail.com
www.tammylagoski.com

Despite the Bumps and Ravines Believe You Are Good Enough

Words all a jumble in my brain, my fingers typing aimlessly seeking the right word, the right vision to tell my story. There are numerous individuals who may not understand why it is so hard to tell the story of finding one's purpose in life; conversely, some folks will understand that not all journeys in life are a joyful and blissful trip, but fraught with bumpy paths of insecurity. Telling the story isn't easy, words sputter and fizzle, until courage triumphs and my soul releases its insecurities and fears to the Holy Spirit. Gently, He reminds me that the journey wasn't always bumpy and full of deep ravines, but filled with expansive and beautiful vistas. Vistas that provided respite, a chance to think and reflect on my purpose in life.

My life started out with chaos, fear, joy and love. It all started when my mother moved to Texas, then met and fell in love with my father. She was the tender age of 15 when they met, and she married him at the age of 16 in Ardmore, Oklahoma. By the time she was 18 years old she was pregnant with me, and my anticipated due date was at the end of October. Like most things in life, plans go awry; thus, my mother was rushed to the Hospital the first of September.

Stubbornly, I refused to cooperate … was breech and wrecking havoc upon my mother's body. The nuns came into my mother's room and discovered to their horror my mother was hemorrhaging. The doctor came in and pronounced my mother had Placenta Previa. The first order of the day was to save the baby at all costs. Pints of blood were fed into my mother's veins, the nuns hurried by her side, placed the sign of the cross on her forehead and proceeded to say the Last Rites over her worn and fragile body.

 Definition of the Last Rites according to American Catholic.Org, "The Catholic Sacrament of Anointing of the Sick, formerly known as Last Rites or Extreme Unction, is a ritual of healing appropriate not only for physical but also for mental and spiritual sickness."

After the Last Rites were performed, the doctor told the nuns to prepare my mother for a Caesarean Section. As my mother struggled to live, the nuns rolled her gurney into the corridor, and thankfully, God heard the prayers of the nuns and so did I; stubbornly, I turned around in the birth canal. Thus, I made my presence known on September 3, 1957 at 11:54 a.m. My mother named me Ina Gynell after my paternal and maternal grandmothers, but my father had other plans. My birth certificate may have said Ina Gynell, but I never heard that name uttered from day one. My father loved the song, "Tammy's in Love," hence my name "Tammy." My father cherished me, always took me with him wherever he went and carried me around the house. Sadly, that soon changed when he and my mother divorced. I was three years old at the time, but I can still remember the love of my father.

Not long after the divorce, my mother moved my two younger brothers and I back to Illinois so we could be near my grandparents. Life percolated on, nothing out of the ordinary happened. We moved into a little apartment where I spent hours playing with the neighbor kids. Since my mother was so poor, we didn't have a car; therefore, we walked everywhere. Rain or shine, I walked to the neighborhood school that was about four blocks away, quite a walk for a little first grader.

As spring gently rolled around, my mother met a gentleman, and by the summer he became my stepfather. Not long after the marriage we moved to the family farm where life was definitely not boring. Second grade was very difficult for me, but by the third grade I found something marvelous … I learned to read! The doors opened, and the world of imagination filtered through my young mind.

Whenever my stepfather came home drunk and abusive, I would hide in my room with books all around me; and if I didn't have books, well, cereal boxes were a great replacement. Thus began my love affair with the printed word. I loved mysteries, silly love stories as well as the stories of Misty and Stormy, the great horses of fiction. Reading was my savior during my stepfather's drunken rages.

Regrettably, there were many more days when I couldn't escape to my room, but had to endure the wrath of my stepfather. He constantly belittled me, told me I was dumb, stupid – basically, I wasn't good enough. On numerous occasions, he delighted in pointing out how smart and gifted my two cousins were. My life was in stark contrast to that of living with a loving father who cherished me, to that of a cold, abusive stepfather. Afraid of making mistakes, afraid of failure, I found it difficult to participate in school activities; for example, reading out loud, spelling bees, music and band. In retrospect, it was probably a good thing I didn't join chorus or play an instrument since I didn't have any rhythm or an ear for music.

In third grade my mother joined First Baptist Church. I loved that church. I made many friends, and blossomed. I also discovered that God loved me regardless of how smart or pretty I was. He loved me for me, nothing more, nothing less, with an unconditional love.

During my sophomore year in high school, I took a Certified Nurse's Assistant (CNA) class. The curriculum required us to work a certain number of hours at the local hospital. Honestly, the chores we were allowed to do were a tad bit boring: filling water pitchers and giving back rubs. To this day, I can still smell the lotion I used on patients during their massages. The real fun and work began when I did my stint as a CNA at the local nursing home.

My placement was on the Skilled Care Wing where most of the patients were bedridden and needed specialized care. I loved working at the nursing home. The nursing home must have loved me, too, as they hired me! I worked for the nursing home until the day I graduated high school. Wow, I thought I had found my calling, my purpose in life.

One day toward the end of my senior year in high school, I met with my counselor and told him I wanted to go to Licensed Practical Nursing (LPN) School. To my utter dismay, he told me I wouldn't make it, that I would fail the classes. My heart was crushed. Yet again, the words permeated my mind, "You aren't good enough or smart enough." Tearfully, heartbroken, I gave up on my dream.

The years went by, I graduated high school, got married the following fall and moved to a new town, a new beginning. I loved being married. There were many ups and downs, but life wasn't too bad. When I wasn't working, I would sit down at my desk and dream about what I would like to be when I grew up (yes, I know, that sounds silly for a grown woman).

One day, I decided to start a prayer journal and document what I would like to accomplish or do with my life. The four "dreams" or goals I wrote down were: be a wife, mother, librarian and a published author.

Obviously, I was a wife, but I still dreamed of being a mother. After seven years of marriage, a miracle happened. I got pregnant and in December of 1982 I gave birth to a beautiful daughter. The year before she was born, I started a new job at the Public Library as a librarian's assistant. I was so happy, yet I still dreamed of being a writer and a Director of the library.

Over the years, I read several books and magazines on writing. While reading Writer's Digest, I noticed that they offered Correspondence courses for Non-Fiction and Fiction writing classes; thus, I enrolled in both classes. Toward the end of my classes, I wrote an article on Fear and Faith. It took me awhile, but I finally mustered up the courage and submitted the manuscript to Guideposts.

After four anxious weeks, I received my first rejection letter. The editor of the magazine checked off the box " ... it wasn't what they were looking for at this time ..." Mr. H. proceeded to write a brief, handwritten message encouraging me in my endeavors of writing. Back in the day, it was the norm to receive a form letter, but not a **handwritten** note. Despite the rejection, I was in heaven; the editor actually sent me a personal note! I still have that rejection letter and treasure it to this day.

After 23 years working at the Library, I had the honor of becoming the Director of the library, another dream come true. I loved that job so very much. Alas, after two years of working at the library, my new husband and I relocated to the southern part of the state. Life should have been happy and joyous, but I had no purpose, no goals. It was hard; I could not find my niche. I lost sight of my purpose.

A year went by, and I still wasn't sure what to do with myself; therefore, I took a huge leap of faith, and I went back to college full time. My major was Psychology, and my goal was to work with the senior population, or become a Grief Counselor for Hospice. I loved my classes, the research, the internships, but sadly, my health took a turn for the worse. I had to have two surgeries, developed various health conditions that put a damper on my education. In the meantime, my husband was cut from his job due to program/financial cuts. I was in my senior year at the university with 24 credits left before I graduated. Yet again, my dreams were dashed and my self-esteem plummeted.

We relocated to central Illinois, which brought us closer to family and friends. In all honesty, I was thankful to be back in central Illinois. But sadly, I felt unsure about my life's purpose. One day, I saw a note on Facebook for an invitation to write a chapter for a multi-author book. After a couple of days of reading the post, I contacted Lisa A Hardwick and asked her about the book, criteria, experience, etc. I took a leap of faith and submitted my manuscript for the book, *Restoring Your Beautiful Life*. Then in a second book, *Step into Your Best Life*, and now this book, *Living Your Purpose*.

The journey to becoming a published author took many years and a lot of blood, sweat and tears. Alas, I was still unsure of my purpose, and what I should do with my life, so I called Sunny Dawn Johnston. We had a long conversation regarding my insecurities and my self-doubts. Talking with Sunny provided clarity and reminded me to believe in self.

 Believe ... within yourself, if you don't you make it hard for you to achieve. Fool yourself if you please, but how can you succeed if you don't believe.

~ TIFFANY COOPER

Sometimes it is still difficult to talk about what I would like to do with my life, just because nothing stays the same. Dreams, goals, and the concept of one's life purpose is constantly changing. I would like to encourage those seeking, feeling self-doubt and unsure of one's purpose in life to stop the chaos and madness and just "be." Don't rush or push yourself for answers; instead, force yourself to be "still" in order to reflect, to dream and reconnect with the soul. Therein lies the answer one seeks to the questions of one's purpose in life.

Please remember, your life purpose may be something as simple as just being – being who you are, who you were meant to be: a soul with love and peace. Not everyone is meant to go tear down mountains, be famous scientists, actors, or authors. The world needs folks to be calm, to be silent nurturers, for it is these folks who are the fabric of everyday life. On the other hand, that does not mean to be complacent and allow events to flow by and control who you become.

As the breech baby in my mother's birth canal, I could have stayed in that position, remained passive, but when my wee ears heard the "Last Rites," I refused to allow someone else to control my fate. Due to pure stubbornness, I turned around and came into this world determined to fight. For a while I allowed the words of my stepfather to echo in my head and truly believed I was not good enough, but as I grew older, the memories and love of my birth father and my Heavenly Father reminded me, yes, I am good enough.

To Alice Lou Gramann, thank you for mentoring and believing in me. Because of you, I fulfilled my dream of becoming a Librarian.

To Mary Downing, my dear friend and mentor. Mary, thank you for believing in me, guiding me and supporting me throughout the years.

To Karen Egan for encouraging me to "Think Outside the Box."

Lastly, to the Illinois State Librarians, who are dedicated in serving the patrons and libraries under their tutelage. I admire and respect you all ...

Thank you to my grandmother, my mother and aunt, who are akin to Lucy and Ethel, and my daughter, Mara. Toss us together, and we become a mass of laughter and tears. Chuck, thank you for loving me and accepting the quirky lady that I am. I love you more than infinity.

~ Tammy Gynell Lagoski

As far as we can discern,
the sole purpose of
human existence is to
kindle a light in the
darkness of mere being.

~ CARL JUNG

Lisa Hardwick

LISA HARDWICK is a Best-Selling Author, Speaker, Workshop Trainer, Publishing Consultant and an advocate for Self Discovery. She is passionate about sharing tools to empower others to live their best lives.

She lives in the same small university town where she was born, Charleston, Illinois, to be near her three adult sons and their families. After years of extensive travel, Lisa learned that her treasure always resided where her journey began.

lisa@lisahardwick.com
www.lisahardwick.com

 Broaden the Scope

What exactly is my purpose and how do I live it? Over the years, I'd wrestle with these questions. I even posed them to others. Finally, one of my favorite spiritual advisors offered some insight. I was told that in order to live your purpose, you must first find your passion. *Find your passion? You mean I have to narrow it down to a single one? Oh no, this is going to be so challenging because I am fascinated by so many things!*

The Passions of a Child

As a child, I was passionate about reading, art, music, dancing, playing make-believe, animals and so many other exciting topics. There were times I would imagine growing up and having an orphanage the children absolutely loved. We would read, paint, sing and dance all day. I would cook wonderful meals for them, bathe them and gently smooth the best lotions money could buy on their little bodies. I would hug them and kiss their cheeks over and over again. At the end of the day, I would tuck each and every one in his or her comfortable little bed while singing lullabies as I went from child to child and assured they felt safe and loved.

Then there were other times I would imagine being a funky-cool art teacher and making a huge difference in the lives of my students by encouraging them to think outside the "square." Every child would have his or her work put on display in a museum – one I had built just for them, and people would travel great distances just to see these professionally framed masterpieces while being served hors d'oeuvres and bubbly champagne as cool jazz music played in the background.

Then there were still other times when I would imagine owning a fifty-acre farm with lots of animals where the pigs, cows and sheep would simply frolic in the pastures until they died from old age. The farmhands and I would groom them, pet and hug them, serve food they enjoyed, and talk to them throughout the day so they were never lonely.

The Unwavering Passions of an Adult

I haven't changed much since I was a child in regards to the things I am passionate about. Even though I no longer fantasize about having a large home for under-privileged children, I *do* know that someday I will travel to Haiti and share my gifts at one of the orphanages I have enthusiastically read about. I know I have the type of soul that will be able to create a space for them simply with my presence where they feel nurtured and loved as well as a place where they are encouraged to grow in alignment with their own individual passions.

To this day, I am known for gathering people together to read, write, learn, sing and dance. I receive messages quite often that ask: *"Hey, Lisa, when is your next get- together?"*

As you can see, I am quite passionate about many things, so instead of trying to pinpoint just *one*, I chose to *broaden the scope* with the awareness of my values and in quintessence, what I cared about the most. Thus, I moved toward those values and then became acutely aware of those opportunities that presented themselves to me – and chose those opportunities that felt most favorable.

Awareness of "The Feeling"

You see, to me, it's all about the feeling. You know, what brings the most joy, what simply feels intuitively good, even the sensation I am vibrating at a high energy level and most importantly, that I am in alignment with my true self. When I have *those* feelings, I know I am living my purpose whether I am planning an event, gathering people for a project to assist with healing the planet or making future plans to visit and assist an orphanage in Haiti.

The question I am most asked is: *"Lisa, what do you think* my *purpose is?"* This is when I suggest what worked for me – to *broaden one's own scope* instead of attempting to pinpoint one specific entity. I may not have the ability to tell someone what his passion and purpose are; however, I *do* know the signs that indicate a person is out of alignment for living a passion-filled and purposeful life. They hate their jobs, their relationships, or their bodies. They don't want to get up in the morning and face a new day. They aren't excited about anything. They are oftentimes depressed or lonely, or both. I know those feelings all too well. I lived a life without purpose many years ago. Quite frankly, it was more exhausting to live that life than to choose to change my focus toward what personally resonated with my true self.

Consider this - if people know what they are passionate about, why do you think they choose not to live their life purposefully? My guess would be perhaps they aren't equipped with the tools to do so or maybe they are fearful to make a change. Perhaps they find it simpler to continue to live a life they hate rather than to take a chance and make changes. I've heard people lament, *"I hate my job!"*, but they were too afraid to make changes so they remained in their rut.

Yes, change can be scary! But embraced with the right attitude, it can be liberating. Do you think it would be more uncomfortable for them to acquire the appropriate tools to eliminate the fear, become brave and simply take a few steps towards what resonates with their true selves or would it feel less distressing to continue to go back to the job they claim to hate? This will be discussed more at the end of this chapter.

The purpose of life is a life of purpose.

~ROBERT BYRNE

We Are All Unique and Purposeful

I am forever grateful I was brave enough to take those first few steps. Was I scared? Oh, you bet! But I was more terrified of waking up and going through life like I had been. Today I make choices daily that are in the flow of what feels right for me. I am also aware that what feels right for *me* most certainly isn't right for *everyone,* and that's a good thing! The planet can only have so many people who do what I do! If everyone did what I do, then who would do the work of a land developer? Who would run the restaurants? Who would craft cute shoes? (I love people who make cute shoes!) The universe is created so perfectly that each being has different and unique passions, which affords each of us a different purpose.

What do you think would happen if everyone lived their lives by doing what they were created to do? If everyone was pursuing his or her passion? If everyone was living a life of purpose? We would be living on a planet that was in beautiful alignment, harmony and replete with amazing energy flow!

 Don't ask yourself what the world needs; ask yourself what makes you come alive. And then go and do that. Because what the world needs is people who have come alive.

~HOWARD THURMAN

Benefits of Living a Life of Purpose

Let's take just a moment and consider what will happen to you as individuals when we choose to focus our energy on our own passions and to live lives of purpose.

1. You will be excited about your day and may experience bouts of euphoria! Can you imagine being excited when you hear the alarm in the morning!?

2. Your work will be fun! I'm not saying your work won't be challenging at times, because it will. However, every hurdle, every obstacle, every hiccup will be worth it!

3. Life in general will flow much more serenely.

4. You will manifest people, things and events in your life that bring you the most joy.

5. You will have more opportunities presented to you that will be in your vibrational flow.

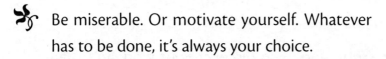 Be miserable. Or motivate yourself. Whatever has to be done, it's always your choice.

~DR. WAYNE DYER

I've learned that singular particularized purpose may change; however, the true passions of your soul seldom do. For example, I absolutely love assisting people with Inner Child Healing. Oh my goodness, it still gives me goose bumps when I teach an individual about taking care of "little you"! To "meet" one's inner child for the first time is magical! To witness the transformation of an adult being guided as to how to nurture, protect and play with his inner child is indescribable. I've met so many beautiful inner children, and I would have to say that has been one of the most rewarding experiences of my life.

When I am conducting Inner Child Healing work – there are times I think that *this* unquestionably is my ultimate purpose. However, when I began writing about Inner Child Healing, it led me to yet another passion and purpose. Writing! And then writing led me to presenting, which led me to assisting other writers and presenters with *their* purposes! Hopefully you now understand my reasoning for *broadening the scope* to your personal values instead of choosing just one specific entity on which to focus.

What is paramount to me is assisting others, and if one of those includes helping him with finding *his* passion and living *his* purpose, then I too am living *my* purpose. I delight in assisting others to discover their best selves and to live their dreams according to their personal values. When I made the conscious choice to *broaden my scope* – an abundance of amazing opportunities were presented to me, and I began building relationships with like-minded people who were in alignment with my true self! (Dear Alarm Clock, feel free to buzz early if you feel so inclined!)

 Your work is to discover your work and then with all your heart to give yourself to it.

~BUDDHA

Your Limited Belief System

Just for a moment, take three deep, cleansing breaths. Now ask yourself, *"If I were living my purpose, who would I be, and what would I be doing?"* Ponder that question for a moment and be aware of how you *feel*. Is your inner spirit experiencing a higher vibration? If so, doesn't that feel absolutely wonderful!?

Perhaps while you were focusing on that question, you heard a small but powerful voice telling you that being that person is unattainable and only a select few are fortunate enough to live that fantasy of living a passion filled and purposeful life. Perhaps the voice whispered to you that you're not talented enough, you don't have the support system or there isn't enough money.

If you *did* hear that message, rest assured the voice is merely a result of your limited belief system. Fear not! That can be changed. Good to know – right? When you become aware of where this "voice" comes from and choose to acknowledge it and move ahead toward your values – you will be moving closer to living a life of purpose.

The next time the limited belief system begins whispering in your ear, smile sweetly and acknowledge it. Then, take hold of your destiny and gently whisk it away while changing your focus and *broaden the scope* of what resonates with your inner being. It is there you will find the passionate and purposeful you.

Dedicated to the beautiful soul I've been anxiously awaiting to meet all my life: my extraordinary granddaughter, Maci Dawn Miller. Also to the many amazing friends, loving and supportive family and the incredibly courageous clients I am fortunate enough to have surrounding me in my life. You bless my life in your own unique way, and I am abundantly grateful for each and every one of you.

To the magnificent teachers who came into my life in many different forms who were instrumental in gently guiding and supporting my ever-growing spiritual development, I thank you. To Nancy Newman, for your dedication to our important purpose and for sharing your incredible talents, I appreciate you!

~ Lisa Hardwick

Profound joy is
like a magnet
that indicates
the path of life.

~ MOTHER TERESA

❧ Resources

The following list of resources are for the national headquarters; search in your yellow pages under "Community Services" for your local resource agencies and support groups.

AIDS

CDC National AIDS Hotline
(800) 342-2437

ALCOHOL ABUSE

Al-Anon Family Group Headquarters
1600 Corporate Landing Parkway
Virginia Beach, VA 23454-5617
(888) 4AL-ANON
www.al-anon.alateen.org

Alcoholics Anonymous (AA)
General Service Office
475 Riverside Dr., 11th Floor
New York, NY 10115
(212) 870-3400
www.alcoholics-anonymous.org

Children of Alcoholics Foundation
164 W. 74th Street
New York, NY 10023
(800) 359-COAF
www.coaf.org

Mothers Against Drunk Driving
MADD
P.O. Box 541688
Dallas, TX 75354
(800) GET-MADD
www.madd.org

National Association of Children of Alcoholics (NACoA)
11426 Rockville Pike, #100
Rockville, MD 20852
(888) 554-2627
www.nacoa.net

Women for Sobriety
P.O. Box 618
Quartertown, PA 18951
(215) 536-8026
www.womenforsobriety.org

CHILDREN'S RESOURCES

Child Molestation

ChildHelp USA/Child Abuse Hotline
15757 N. 78th St.
Scottsdale, AZ 85260
(800) 422-4453
www.childhelpusa.org

Prevent Child Abuse America
200 South Michigan Avenue, 17th Floor
Chicago, IL 60604
(312) 663-3520
www.preventchildabuse.org

Crisis Intervention

Girls and Boys Town National Hotline
(800) 448-3000
www.boystown.org

Children's Advocacy Center of East Central Illinois
*(If your heart feels directed to make a donation to this center,
please include Lisa Hardwick's name in the memo)*
616 6th Street
Charleston, IL 61920
(217) 345-8250
http://caceci.org

Children of the Night
14530 Sylvan St.
Van Nuys, CA 91411
(800) 551-1300
www.childrenofthenight.org

National Children's Advocacy Center
210 Pratt Avenue
Huntsville, AL 35801
(256) 533-KIDS (5437)
www.nationalcac.org

Co-Dependency

Co-Dependents Anonymous
P.O. Box 33577
Phoenix, AZ 85067
(602) 277-7991
www.codependents.org

Suicide, Death, Grief

AARP Grief and Loss Programs
(800) 424-3410
www.aarp.org/griefandloss

Grief Recovery Institute
P.O. Box 6061-382
Sherman Oaks, CA 91413
(818) 907-9600
www.grief-recovery.com

Suicide Awareness Voices of Education
Minneapolis, MN 55424
(952) 946-7998

Suicide National Hotline
(800) 784-2433

DOMESTIC VIOLENCE

National Coalition Against Domestic Violence
P.O. Box 18749
Denver, CO 80218
(303) 831-9251
www.ncadv.org

National Domestic Violence Hotline
P.O. Box 161810
Austin, TX 78716
(800) 799-SAFE
www.ndvh.org

DRUG ABUSE

Cocaine Anonymous National Referral Line
(800) 347-8998

National Helpline of Phoenix House
(800) COCAINE
www.drughelp.org

National Institute of Drug Abuse
(NIDA)
6001 Executive Blvd., Room 5213,
Bethesda, MD 20892-9561, Parklawn
Building
Info: (301) 443-6245
Help: (800) 662-4357
www.nida.nih.gov

EATING DISORDERS

Overeaters Anonymous
National Office
P.O. Box 44020
Rio Rancho, NM 87174-4020
(505) 891-2664
www.overeatersanonymous.org

GAMBLING

Gamblers Anonymous
International Service Office
P.O. Box 17173
Los Angeles, CA 90017
(213) 386-8789
www.gamblersanonymous.org

HEALTH ISSUES

American Chronic Pain Association
P.O. Box 850
Rocklin, CA 95677
(916) 632-0922
www.theacpa.org

American Holistic Health Association
P.O. Box 17400
Anaheim, CA 92817
(714) 779-6152
www.ahha.org

The Chopra Center at La Costa Resort and Spa Deepak Chopra, M.D.
2013 Costa Del Mar
Carlsbad, CA 92009
(760) 494-1600
www.chopra.com

The Mind-Body Medical Institute
110 Francis St., Ste. 1A
Boston, MA 02215
(617) 632-9530 Ext. 1
www.mbmi.org

National Health Information Center
P.O. Box 1133
Washington, DC 20013-1133
(800) 336-4797
www.health.gov/NHIC

Preventive Medicine Research Institute
Dean Ornish, M.D.
900 Brideway, Ste 2
Sausalito, CA 94965
(415) 332-2525
www.pmri.org

MENTAL HEALTH

American Psychiatric Association of America
1400 K St. NW
Washington, DC 20005
(888) 357-7924
www.psych.org

Anxiety Disorders Association of America
11900 Parklawn Dr., Ste. 100
Rockville, MD 20852
(310) 231-9350
www.adaa.org

The Help Center of the American Psychological Association
(800) 964-2000
www.helping.apa.org

National Center for Post Traumatic Stress Disorder
(802) 296-5132
www.ncptsd.org

National Alliance for the Mentally Ill
2107 Wilson Blvd., Ste. 300
Arlington, VA 22201
(800) 950-6264
www.nami.org

National Depressive and Manic-Depressive Association
730 N. Franklin St., Ste. 501
Chicago, IL 60610
(800) 826-3632
www.ndmda.org

National Institute of Mental Health
6001 Executive Blvd.
Room 81884, MSC 9663
Bethesda, MD 20892
(301) 443-4513
www.nimh.nih.gov

SEX ISSUES

Rape, Abuse and Incest
National Network
(800) 656-4673
www.rainn.org

National Council on Sexual Addiction
and Compulsivity
P.O. Box 725544
Atlanta, GA 31139
(770) 541-9912
www.ncsac.org

SMOKING

Nicotine Anonymous World Services
419 Main St., PMB #370
Huntington Beach, CA 92648
(415) 750-0328
www.nicotine-anonymous.org

STRESS ISSUES

The Biofeedback & Psychophysiology Clinic
The Menninger Clinic
P.O. Box 829
Topeka, KS 66601-0829
(800) 351-9058
www.menninger.edu

New York Open Center
83 Spring St.
New York, NY 10012
(212) 219-2527
www.opencenter.org

The Stress Reduction Clinic Center for Mindfulness
University of Massachusetts
Medical Center
55 Lake Ave., North
Worcester, MA 01655
(508) 856-2656

TEEN

Al-Anon/Alateen
1600 Corporate Landing Parkway
Virginia Beach, VA 23454-5617
(888) 425-2666
www.al-anon.alateen.org

Planned Parenthood
810 Seventh Ave.
New York, NY 10019
(800) 230-PLAN
www.plannedparenthood.org

Hotlines for Teenagers
Girls and Boys Town National Hotline
(800) 448-3000

ChildHelp National Child Abuse Hotline
(800) 422-4453

Just for Kids Hotline
(888) 594-KIDS

National Child Abuse Hotline
(800) 792-5200

National Runaway Hotline
(800) 621-4000

National Youth Crisis Hotline
(800)-HIT-HOME

Suicide Prevention Hotline
(800) 827-7571

A Call For Authors

Most people have a story that needs to be shared – could **YOU** be one of the contributing authors we are seeking to feature in one of our upcoming books?

Whether you envision yourself participating in an inspiring book with other authors, or whether you have a dream of writing your very own book, we may be the answer **YOU** have been searching for!

Are you interested in experiencing how sharing your message will assist with building your business network, which in turn will result in being able to assist even more people? Or perhaps you are interested in leaving a legacy for your family and friends? Or it may be you simply have an important message your heart is telling you to share with the world. Each person has their own unique reason for desiring to become an author.

Our commitment is to make this planet we call "home" a better place. One of the ways we fulfill this commitment is assisting others in sharing their inspiring messages.

We look forward to hearing from you.

Please visit us at
www.visionaryinsightpress.com

Lightning Source UK Ltd.
Milton Keynes UK
UKOW04f0252131113

220956UK00001B/12/P